Into All the World

What the Bible teaches
about mission

Norman A. Shields

BRYNTIRION PRESS

© Norman A. Shields 1998
First published 1998
ISBN 1 85049 144 5

Published by Bryntirion Press
Bryntirion, Bridgend CF31 4DX, Wales, UK
Printed by Creative Print and Design, Ebbw Vale

Contents

'Go and make disciples of all nations,
baptising them in the name of the Father
and of the Son and of the Holy Spirit,
and teaching them to obey
everything I have commanded you.
And surely I am with you always,
to the very end of the age.'
Matthew 28:19-20

Foreword

As the son of missionary parents, I well remember the banners around the walls of the missionary conventions I used to attend in my childhood and youth in Northern Ireland. All the best missionary texts were on them: 'Go ye into all the world and preach the gospel to every creature'; 'Go ye therefore and make disciples of all nations'. They were all from the New Testament, of course, and they all seemed to come from the back ends of the Gospels, almost as much of an afterthought for Jesus as mission seemed to be an optional extra for many other Christians. However, for those of us brought up to respect those climactic texts as 'The Great Commission', it was enough that Jesus had commanded it. Mission was of the essence of what it meant to be a committed, obedient Christian. For some of us, mission was in the blood anyway.

Only later in life did I realize how central and pervasive was the reality of mission in the whole of the Scriptures. This truth dawned on me, not, regrettably, in the days of my theological education (during which I do not recall that mission or missiology ever made an appearance in the official curriculum), nor even in the days of my pastoral ministry in an English parish. It happened when I found myself as a tutor in Old Testament studies teaching men and women who were training for cross-cultural mission at All Nations Christian College in 1982, before I went to do the same task in India. 'What relevance', I asked myself as I prepared to teach various OT books, 'do these biblical texts have for Christian mission?' The answers staggered me. I rediscovered the mission of the biblical God himself, the God who created humanity with a mission on earth, who called Abraham with the ultimate mission of blessing all the nations of th earth through his descendants, who shaped Israel to be a model to the nations of what God's idea of redemption looks like, who sent his Son with a sense of identity and mission that was profoundly shaped by the missionary message of his own Scriptures (our OT), and who initiated through the church a mission to the Gentiles that will eventually fulfil the promise to Abraham, when people from every nation, language, tribe and people gather before the throne of God and of the Lamb. The whole Bible is a witness to the mission of God, and addresses the people of God in their missionary engagement with God's world.

The task of expounding the full missiological content and significance of the Bible would be enormous and far beyond the scope of this book, but Norman Shields enables readers to take the first steps in that direction. This book is a helpful basic introduction to some of the biblical foundations for mission. I trust it will help many to discover more quickly than I did that mission is the heartbeat of God and of God's Word. And I trust they will then go on to read and to preach the Bible from that perspective.

Rev. Dr Chris Wright
Principal, All Nations Christian College

Preface

It was in the winter of 1963-4 that I first met the Reverend David Kingdon, who had recently become Principal of the Irish Baptist College. I had been serving with the Qua Iboe Mission in West Africa for twelve years, but because of family responsibilities was then its Deputation Secretary based in Belfast. Mr Kingdon asked me if I would be willing to teach Missionary Principles in the following year.

From September 1964 till Easter 1965 I taught a two-term series of lectures which began with a survey of the Biblical Basis of Mission. In the autumn of 1966 I joined the staff at the College and Missiology became and remained one of my courses till I retired in 1990. Since then I have been privileged to continue teaching the biblical section of the College's Missiology course. Needless to say the material used in those lectures is the basis of what has been written for this book.

I am grateful to my friend of the past 35 years, David Kingdon, and to the publishers, for whom he now serves as Managing Editor, for the opportunity to make this material more widely available.

My prayer is that the Lord will use this book to bring home to many the biblical nature of the responsibility resting on Christians to make Christ known. The Lord expects his followers to be his witnesses in terms that admit of no alternative: 'You will be my witnesses . . .' Christians and the churches to which they belong are not just required to be interested in but to be participants in mission. There is abiding truth in the slogan one used to hear in the 1970s, 'the church is mission'. It is, of course, more than mission, but when it is not involved in mission it is seriously open to question if it is a church in the New Testament sense of the term.

Jesus said, '. . . you will be my witnesses in Jerusalem, and in all Judea and Samaria, and to the ends of the earth' (Acts 1:8).

Introduction

We use the word 'mission' of virtually any form of Christian outreach. It is derived from the Latin verb *mittere* meaning 'to send'. Mission is a 'sending out' and a missionary is someone who has been sent to (or commissioned for) a specific task.

The word is closely connected with another that is familiar to Christians, the word 'apostle'. This comes from the Greek verb *apostello* which means 'to send out' and which was often translated into Latin by *mittere* (e.g. Matt.10:16,40). An apostle is essentially, then, a sent or sent-out person, a missionary.

It needs to be remembered, however, that the disciples who were commissioned as apostles by our Lord himself were witnesses of his entire ministry and of his death and resurrection. In Acts 1:21f. we have a record of how Peter spelled out these qualifications in connection with the finding of a successor to Judas. The fact that the disciples had been with Jesus for some three years and were first-hand witnesses of his life and work gave them a unique authority in terms of knowing and passing on the facts about him and of being the founding fathers of the church. In this sense they were unique, the APOSTLES.

At the same time the New Testament uses the word 'apostle' of a wide variety of folk who participated in the work of mission. Barnabas is called an 'apostle' (Acts 14:4,14) and James, the brother of our Lord, also seems to have been regarded as such (Gal. 1:19). Andronicus and Junia are said to have been 'outstanding among the apostles' (Rom. 16:7). Two unnamed Christians are called apostles (Greek, *apostoloi*) in 2 Corinthians 8:23. The Authorised Version refers to these two as 'messengers' while the New International Version uses 'representatives'. Both translations catch something of the fact that the two men concerned had been sent on a mission by the Macedonian churches—they were

11

missionaries or 'apostles' without being among those we have designated the APOSTLES.

The position of Paul is interesting, because he was not an eyewitness of the ministry, death and resurrection of the Lord. He was not one of the twelve. Yet he was unique in that the risen Lord had appeared to him and had commissioned him to be an apostle (Acts 9:1-22, 26:12-18). He saw himself as an apostle (Rom. 1:1; 11:13; 1 Cor. 1:1; 9:1; 15:9; 1 Tim. 2:7; 2 Tim. 1:11 etc.) and always sought to fulfil the commission that had been given to him. In a sense Paul can be considered as a bridge between the original APOSTLES, the twelve, and the broader spectrum of helpers in mission who are also designated apostles.

The New Testament speaks of the church being blessed with persons called 'apostles' who were, apparently, 'gifted' to serve in that role (1 Cor. 12:28f.; Eph. 4:11). The question of whether or not the same gift is still bestowed is often quite divisive today. There are denominations—and cults—which appoint apostles, usually twelve in number, and give them authority over the denomination. They regard apostleship in the capital-letter sense of the original twelve as still part of God's plan. Catholicism with its doctrine of apostolic succession applies this to bishops and interprets it in terms of hierarchical authority.

Biblically orientated Christians generally regard the capital-letter APOSTLES as being without successors and therefore irreplaceable—there can be no new witnesses to our Lord's ministry. But they see the secondary sense of the word apostle as of abiding validity with reference to evangelists and missionaries, i.e., to all those who spread the gospel, who teach what the Lord taught and who plant churches.

In effect the APOSTOLIC *office* has ceased, but the apostolic *function* of mission continues as the Lord calls whom he wills to serve him; and as his churches send such persons out into the world as missionaries to persuade individuals to turn to Christ and to plant churches. It is with this apostolic or missionary function that we concern ourselves in the studies that follow.

12

1
The Sovereign Initiator

The Christian doctrine of mission has its roots in the revelation of God and of his purposes in the Old Testament.

The primary focus is on its teaching about God himself, but the records of the calling and commissioning of individuals to serve him in tasks of a specifically missionary nature are also important.

The Lord is universally sovereign

From Genesis to Malachi the Lord is presented as the Creator of all that exists. The first two chapters of Genesis provide the only record of creation available to us, but many other passages also attribute it to God, the LORD. For example:

> You alone are the LORD. You made the heavens, even the highest heavens, and all their starry host, the earth and all that is on it, the seas and all that is in them. You give life to everything and the multitudes of heaven worship you (Neh. 9:6; cf. Deut. 4:32; Ps. 148:5; Isa. 40:26; Mal. 2:10).

As Creator of all the Lord alone is God—'The LORD is God in heaven above, and on the earth below. There is no other' (Deut. 4:39; cf. 1 Kgs. 8:60; Isa. 44:6-20, etc.). In addition, as the source of all that exists, God is the ultimate owner of everything—'The earth is the LORD's, and everything in it, the world, and all who live in it' (Ps. 24:1). As David said in a great prayer, The Lord is the one to whom 'everything in heaven and earth' belongs, the one who is 'exalted as head over all' and who is 'the ruler of all things' (1 Chr. 29:11-12). His ownership and his sovereignty

13

therefore extend to the whole of creation—he is universally sovereign.

Despite the fact that the Old Testament is essentially about God's relationship to and his sovereignty over his covenant people, Israel, his sovereignty over all nations was also asserted. On the ground of his universal sovereignty he required the submission and allegiance of all his creatures. This requirement is implicit in the repeated castigation and punishment of the moral failures of the nations that surrounded Israel:

I will punish the king of Assyria for the wilful pride of his heart and the haughty look in his eyes . . . The LORD . . . will send a wasting disease upon his sturdy warriors; under his pomp a fire will be kindled like a blazing flame . . . The splendour of his forests and fertile fields it will completely destroy . . . (Isa. 10:16,18; cf. Isa. 13–21,23; Joel 3; Nah. 1–3; Hab. 2; Zeph. 2:4-15).

1. His sovereignty was to be recognised
a) *By Israel, God's covenant people*
The Israelites themselves were often guilty of pursuing a way of life that was out of harmony with God's purposes for them. In the Judges period every one was doing as he saw fit (Judg. 17:6), and in the period of the monarchy the nation again and again departed from the Lord. They mixed, or rather tried to mix, the worship of God with the worship of and allegiance to Baal. In God's eyes this was the same as forsaking him and was just not acceptable to the Lord—it had to be one or the other. Hence Elijah's great challenge on Mount Carmel, 'if the LORD is God, follow him; but if Baal is God, follow him (1 Kgs. 18:21). Despite that challenge the worship of Baal continued and was the major factor in the demise of the northern kingdom of Israel and in the exile of Judah. The Lord's people were not submitting to his sovereignty.

The abandonment of social justice is a recurring theme in the prophets and is another indication of the nation's lack of submission to the Lord. Amos, for example, insisted that injustice was a sin against a righteous God, in effect a rejection of his sovereign rule. He addressed his hearers as those who 'turn justice into bitterness and cast righteousness to the ground' (5:7) and even castigated women who oppressed the poor, who crushed the needy and who lorded it over their husbands (4:1). He wanted justice to roll on like a river (5:24) and envisaged a day when, after the punishment of the exile, the Lord would bring back and establish his people on a permanent basis. For Amos and, indeed, all the prophets, restoration would mean submission to the Lord's sovereignty.

b) *By non-Israelite nations*
The Old Testament often demands that men everywhere submit to the sovereign rule of the Lord. This demand was implicit in those passages in which the prophets condemned the cruelties and injustices of foreign nations and is clearly explicit in many of the psalms. Thus Psalm 2, predicting that God's Son would be given the nations for his inheritance and would rule over them with an iron sceptre, calls on earthly rulers to 'serve the LORD with fear' and to 'kiss the Son, lest he be angry' (vv. 10-12). That is a call to submit to the Lord as sovereign.

In Psalm 66 the whole earth is urged to sing to the glory of God's name and to offer him glory and praise (vv. 1-2). The next psalm (67) opens with a prayer that God's ways might be known on earth and his salvation among all nations. It goes on to pray that the peoples and nations of the world may join with those God blesses in Israel to praise the Lord and to fear him—'God will bless us and all the ends of the earth will fear him' (67:7). Again the submission of the Lord's own people to his sovereign authority is in view, and it is clearly a goal which God expected his people to espouse and in the achievement of which they had a part to play. It was an aspect of the reason for their existence as God's people and an important element in their mission to the rest of his world.

2. His sovereignty was to be proclaimed
In Psalm 96 God's people are asked to 'declare his glory among the nations, his marvellous deeds among all peoples' (v. 3). They

are to 'say among the nations, "The LORD reigns,"' (v. 10). Psalm 145 also shows that the Lord, who is good and gracious, has what we, in the light of the New Testament revelation, would call a missionary concern. His saints will, it says, 'tell of the glory of your kingdom and speak of your might, so that all men may know of your mighty acts and the glorious splendour of your kingdom' (vv. 11-12).

When Solomon dedicated the temple he expressed a concern that foreigners would come there to pray and he asked the Lord to hear and respond to their prayers. This again was a missionary concern:

Do whatever the foreigner asks of you, so that all the peoples of the earth may know your name and fear you, as do your people, Israel, and may know that this house that I have built bears your Name (1 Kgs. 8:43; cf. v. 60).

Associated with this expectation that God's sovereignty should be proclaimed is the fact that the Lord's own people were often rebuked for behaviour which profaned rather than honoured his name and which turned men of other races away from him. By the punishment he imposed on them, he would bring the nations to realise that he was indeed the Lord.

I poured out my wrath on them [i.e., the Israelites/the Jews] . . . I dispersed them among the nations . . . I judged them according to their conduct . . . I had concern for my holy name, which the house of Israel profaned . . . Therefore . . . I will show the holiness of my great name, which has been profaned among the nations, the name you have profaned among them. Then the nations will know that I am the LORD, declares the Sovereign LORD, when I show myself holy through you before their eyes (Ezek. 36:18-23).

It is also relevant that the message Jonah proclaimed to the people of Nineveh called on them to repent and in so doing proclaimed

16

God's sovereignty over them. That they (from the king to the lowest citizen) repented involved a considerable degree of submission to the sovereign authority of God, the Lord (Jon. 3:6-10).

Clearly, then, the Old Testament proclaims God's sovereign rule and calls on all men everywhere to submit to that rule.

3. His sovereignty would be accepted
The prophets predicted that ultimately all mankind would submit to the sovereign rule of God, the Lord. Isaiah, for example, looked forward to a day when many peoples would come to the house of the Lord and say,

> Come, let us go up to the mountain of the LORD, to the house of the God of Jacob. He will teach us his ways, so that we may walk in his paths (2:3).

The picture is of Gentiles spontaneously turning to the Lord, because the mountain of the Lord's temple would be established as chief among the mountains (v. 2). This imagery seems to mean that the reputation of God the Lord would be enhanced so as to draw multitudes to himself and to espousal of his ways.

The same idea occurs several times in Isaiah's prophecy. In one passage the Lord says, 'foreigners who bind themselves to the LORD to serve him . . . I will bring to my holy mountain' (56:6,7). In the very last chapter of the book God asserted that he would 'gather all nations and tongues' to see his glory and to become proclaimers of that glory and, in some cases, to minister alongside Israelites (66:18-21).

In the Servant Songs of Isaiah 40-56 God's Servant is presented as commissioned to express his universal sovereignty by bringing justice to the nations (42:1,4). The Servant would also be a light to the nations to ensure that God's salvation would reach the ends of the earth (49:6). In the same section of the book the very ends of the earth were challenged to turn to the Lord in order to be saved, and this message was affirmed by a divine oath which proclaimed the ultimate sovereignty of the Lord over all humanity.

> By myself I have sworn,
>   my mouth has uttered in all integrity
>   a word that will not be revoked:
> Before me every knee will bow;
>   by me every tongue will swear.
>
> > (Isa. 45:23)

The ultimate sovereignty of God with the subjection of all opposing forces is, indeed, clearly predicted in the Old Testament. What is and always has been a fact—that God is universally sovereign—will one day be universally acknowledged.

The Lord's perfect righteousness

When Scripture speaks of the Lord as righteous it is saying that his character and behaviour conform to a standard of right which arises within his own being. To that standard he is always true. There is no inconsistency between what he is in his moral nature and what he does in his relationships with his creatures. He, the righteous Lord, 'the Judge of all the earth', does right (Gen. 18:25; cf. Ezr. 9:15; Pss. 19:8; 116:5; Isa. 45:24; Jer. 9:24b; 12:1; Hos. 14:9b, etc.).

This being so it follows that the demands he makes on men are also righteous,

> Righteous are you, O LORD,
>   and your laws are right.
> The statutes you have laid down are righteous;
>   they are fully trustworthy.
>
> > (Ps. 119:137f.)
>
> All his ways are just.
> > (Deut. 32:4; cf. 2 Chr. 12:6; Ps. 99:4)

Justice is righteousness in action, giving men and women their due deserts. Because God is righteous (or just), he always responds to human behaviour in ways that conform to his character. For example,

1. He reacts against sin and punishes its perpetrators

If God did not react to sin he would be discriminating against the righteous! That he does react means that unforgiven sinners are liable to his wrath—'he does not leave the guilty unpunished' (Ex. 34:7; Nah. 1:3,6, etc.).

2. He saves the oppressed and the believing

His righteousness is active rather than passive. He acts to deliver those who are oppressed and who trust in him. Thus in righteousness he would raise up Cyrus, king of Persia, to free the Jews oppressed in Babylon—he is at once a righteous God and a Saviour (Isa. 45:13,21; 46:12-13, etc.).

3. He demands repentance

The prophets called for this both at the personal and at the national levels. There was nothing men or nations could do to eradicate the stain of sin and gain acceptance with God. They must repent and seek God's forgiveness,

> Although you wash yourself with soda
> and use an abundance of soap,
> the stain of your guilt is still before me
> declares the Sovereign LORD.
>
> (Jer. 2:22)

The Israelites faced calamity unless they genuinely abandoned their sin and turned or returned to the Lord (Isa. 1:16-20; 30:15-18; 65:1-6; Jer. 3:11-14; 18:1-11; Hos. 6:1-3; 14:1-9; Amos 5:4-8, etc.).

4. He justifies the repentant

Repentance is not merely the abandonment of sin but a positive turning to and dependence on (or faith in) the Lord. Abraham's acceptance with God lay in the fact that he believed or trusted God—'Abraham believed the LORD, and he [the Lord] credited it to him as righteousness' (Gen. 15:6). This means that Abraham had a righteous status before God—he was justified.

The Psalmist, rejoicing in the fact that his sins had been forgiven, also saw himself in a new and right relationship with the Lord:

> Blessed is he
>   whose transgressions are forgiven,
>   whose sins are covered . . .
> whose sin the Lord does not count against him. . . .
> Then I acknowledged my sin to you
>   and did not cover up my iniquity.
> I said, 'I will confess
>   my transgressions to the LORD'—
> and you forgave
>   the guilt of my sin.
> Therefore let everyone who is godly pray to you
>   while you may be found . . .
>
> (Ps. 32:1-6; cf. Ps. 51:13-17)

In both psalms the writer enthused because he had experienced justification through God's forgiving and restoring grace. That there was such grace, that forgiven sinners could enjoy a proper relationship with God, is a theological fact of immense significance. That it appears in the Old Testament shows how God was preparing for the coming of Christ and for a Christian mission in which 'justification by faith' would be absolutely central and would be the only way to enjoy forgiveness and eternal salvation.

The Lord plans to bless all races

When he called Abram, the Lord promised that all the peoples on earth would be blessed through him (Gen. 12:3). This promise was repeated to both Isaac and Jacob (Gen. 26:4; 28:14) and, despite a parallel emphasis on Israelites keeping themselves separate from pagan peoples, was never forgotten. The Israelites were told that though the Lord loved them in a special way they must not think of themselves as more righteous than other peoples—'it is not because of your righteousness that the Lord your

God is giving you this good land . . . for you are a stiff-necked people' (Deut. 9:4-6; cf. 7:7-8; 10:15).

The Israelites were also given laws insisting that foreigners were not to be ill-treated or oppresed—'Do not ill-treat an alien or oppress him, for you were aliens in Egypt' (Ex. 22:21). Indeed foreigners were to be treated as if they were natives:

> The alien living with you must be treated as one of your native-born. Love him as yourself, for you were aliens in Egypt. I am the LORD your God (Lev. 19:34).

As an expression of this requirement the gleanings of the fields and the vineyards were to be left for the poor and the stranger (Lev. 19:10; Deut. 24:14-22). This showed a positive concern for the well-being of needy people whether they were Israelite and non-Israelite. The latter were also God's creatures and worthy of the same respect and love as were Israelites.

That the Israelites failed to fulfil these requirements does not detract from the fact that God intended non-Israelites to be properly treated. His promise to Ebed-Melech, who had saved Jeremiah's life, exemplifies his care of an Ethiopian slave, whose life many would have considered expendable (Jer. 38:7-13; 39:15-18).

In the teachings of the prophets there arose the idea of a new covenant, a new basis on which God would relate to his people (Jer. 31:27-34; Ezek. 36:25-37:14; Joel 2:25-32). In the context the Lord was addressing 'the house of Israel' but, as the New Testament shows, the new covenant was inaugurated in Christ— 'this is my blood of the covenant' (Matt. 26:28).

The new covenant promise was that God's Spirit would be poured out on all people and not just on Israelites (Joel 2:28; cf. Acts 2:18 for the fulfilment). The new covenant relationship was, therefore, to be the privilege of the redeemed of all races. In its fulfilment it is just that—men 'from every tribe and . . . nation' (Rev. 5:9, etc.) are called into the service of God.

God's purposes of blessing really do reach out to all places and to all peoples.

2

The prophets as missionaries

The Old Testament abounds with instances of God calling people to fulfil specific commissions both to their fellow Israelites and to Gentile races.

Those called to such service are usually known as prophets, but occasionally the ordinary Hebrew word for messenger *(malak)* is used. Haggai is called 'the LORD's messenger' whose function was to pass on the 'message of the LORD to the people' (Hag. 1:13). Malachi looked forward to John the Baptist as the Lord's 'messenger' who would prepare the way for him (Mal. 3:1; cf. Mark 1:1-8).

The prophets, then, were missionary messengers. They were sent by God and they spoke for God and delivered his word to those he wanted to receive it. Their mission was to proclaim God's truth.

The early prophets

1. Moses
The first instance of the Lord commissioning someone to act as his spokesman occurred towards the end of the Israelites' sojourn in Egypt. He appeared to Moses at the burning bush and commissioned him to lead Israel out of Egypt—'Go. I am sending you to Pharaoh to bring my people the Israelites out of Egypt' (Ex. 3:10). He was told what to say to the people, to their elders and to Pharaoh, but he was afraid and prevaricated considerably. Eventually the Lord told him that his brother Aaron would act as his spokesman or prophet (Ex. 4:15f.; 7:1). Moses and Aaron had a shared mission—they were both missionaries but, as time went on, their functions changed.

While Aaron was commissioned to operate as head of the nation's priesthood, Moses was essentially God's spokesman-prophet. He delivered the commandments and the larger body of Mosaic law and was in a sense the greatest prophet of the Old Testament era. He was the only one ever privileged to present his own ministry as a picture or type of the ministry of 'The Supreme Prophet' of all time—'The LORD your God will raise up for you a prophet like me . . .' (Deut. 18:15-18). He was certainly unique in the early period and probably also in the whole Old Testament era (Deut. 34:10).

2. Samuel

Samuel was dominant in the transition from the period of the Judges to that of the monarchy. The story of his call to service (1 Sam. 1–3) is well-known—he heard God calling him by name and responded with the words, 'Speak, for your servant is listening' (3:10). His first message was one of rebuke for his earthly master Eli (3:11-14), but soon he was recognised throughout Israel as a messenger or prophet of the Lord (3:19–4:1). It was his privilege to anoint Saul to be the first king of Israel and, when the Lord rejected Saul, to seek out and anoint David to be his successor. Throughout a long ministry he was the Lord's messenger, his missionary to Israel. On his death he was mourned throughout the land (25:1).

3. Elijah and Elisha

Elijah, whose name means, 'the Lord is my God', appeared on the scene in the days of Ahab, a particularly evil king who reigned in the ninth century BC. His first task was to announce a period of drought, which seems to have been divine punishment for the wickedness of the time. During the reigns of Ahab and his successor Ahaziah, he made a number of forays into the public domain to assert the claims of the Lord as against those of the Baals who were then so widely honoured in Israel. He was a charismatic representative of the Lord who confronted the king and the prophets of Baal. On one occasion, however, he fled from Jezebel, Ahab's Baal-worshipping wife, and, thinking that he alone had stood firm for the Lord, was sliding into despair (1 Kgs. 19). From Horeb where he had taken refuge the Lord sent Elijah back to Israel by the way he had come and told him to recruit Elisha as his successor. As he went he found Elisha ploughing and to assure him of his intention to take him as his companion threw his cloak around him (v. 19). Significantly when Elijah was translated his cloak replaced Elisha's own (2 Kgs. 2:11ff.).

The younger man, Elisha, responded to the call of Elijah (and of the Lord) by farewelling his parents, slaughtering his oxen, burning his farming equipment and following Elijah as his attendant. There were no half measures with Elisha. To fulfil his mission he forsook his family and his means of livelihood and committed himself totally to his new calling. Many years later when Elijah died his mantle fell on Elisha, who like his master was used to perform miracles as signs of the Lord's presence and continuing sovereignty. He seems to have been a milder character than Elijah but, like him, was thoroughly faithful in fulfilling God's commission.

The writing prophets

In a number of instances we have interesting records of how the Lord brought the prophets into his service, and commissioned them for specific tasks.

1. Isaiah

In the case of Isaiah there seems to have been a period of prophetic ministry (chapters 1–5) before the special commission recorded in chapter 6 was received. On that occasion Isaiah was caught up in a vision of the Lord enthroned high up in or above the temple. He was inwardly shattered by the vision, in which the majesty and the absolute holiness of the Lord were clearly presented to him (v. 3). In comparison he saw himself as ruined because of his uncleanness and the uncleanness of his people.

He also saw himself by the grace of God receiving cleansing from his sin. Then he heard the Lord's challenge, 'Whom shall I send? And who will go for us?' His response was unequivocal, 'Here am I. Send me!' (v. 8). And thereupon he became a missionary, one sent to proclaim the Lord's message to Judah.

Isaiah's task was to tell his people some unpalatable truths and to pinpoint their unwillingness and inability to respond to God's word (vv. 9,10). Evidently this was not totally congenial to the prophet, who seems to have realised that it meant spending years and years beating his head against the stone wall of his hearers' obduracy. He asked, as anyone in such a situation might ask, 'For how long, O Lord?'

The answer he received (vv. 11-13) has some enigmatic elements to it, but meant that he would have to go on and on preaching to unresponsive people for the rest of what as a young man he could expect to be, and what was in fact, a long life. That was his mission. It is to his credit that he kept at it even though he saw no outward results for his labours.

2. Jeremiah

Jeremiah's call came through a verbal revelation from God— 'The word of the LORD came to me . . .' (Jer. 1:4). He was told that he had been chosen to be a prophet to the nations but, like Moses centuries earlier, he argued that he didn't have the speaking skills needed to be the Lord's messenger. But the Lord continued to work in his life and was soon using him as a messenger or missionary to Judah.

During his ministry he went through many difficult experiences. He, alone of all the servants of God whose stories appear in Scripture, was told that he was not to marry (16:2). This was because of the traumatic suffering hanging over Judah at the time, which has parallels with the advice against marriage given by Paul in 1 Corinthians 7:26. The difference is that Jeremiah was under a divine command, while Paul only gave advice and admitted that he had *no* command from the Lord about the matter. Jeremiah was a man of deep emotion, who was often driven to tears because of the folly and the impending fate of his people:

> Since my people are crushed, I am crushed;
> I mourn, and horror grips me . . .
> Oh, that my head were a spring of water
> and my eyes a fountain of tears!

> I would weep day and night
>> for the slain of my people.
>>> (Jer. 8:21–9:1)

Like Isaiah before him, Jeremiah saw little by way of a positive response to his message. But he had a commission from the Lord, and to the end of his ministry he continued to tell his people 'all the words of the LORD their God' (43:1). In addition he also received and delivered messages from the Lord for the nations that surrounded and impinged on Judah (46:1–51:64). He was a missionary sent both to Judah and to those pagan nations.

3. Ezekiel

Ezekiel, who prophesied among the Jews exiled in Babylon, was also clearly called by the Lord to his life-work (2:1-10). He was told to speak God's words to his people, whether they would listen or not, and not to be afraid of what they would say to him. His ministry was to be solely to his own people: 'You are not being sent to a people of obscure speech and difficult language, but to the house of Israel' (3:5).

He was to be a 'watchman for the house of Israel'. His mission was to warn them of spiritual and moral dangers (Ezek. 3:17; cf. 33:7). Despite considerable adversity, he was faithful to this commission. He acted as a watchman and, in addition to delivering words of rebuke, was privileged to look forward and offer new hope to his people (Ezek. 36:24–37:14 etc.).

4. Amos

Amos was a shepherd and fig-tree cultivator in the northern kingdom of Israel and did not regard himself as a prophet or the son of a prophet (i.e., not a member of a prophetic school like those operating in the times of Samuel and Elijah). He says, 'The LORD took me from tending the flock and said to me, "Go, prophesy to my people Israel"' (Amos 7:14,15).

Here, then, was a simple shepherd boy who was called by the Lord and used by him to bring his message not just to Israel

27

but to a group of neighbouring nations (1:3–2:5). He seems to have been somewhat amazed that the Lord should have chosen him for such tasks, but he gained confidence and was able to address king Amaziah with the authority of a man sent from God,

'Your wife will become a prostitute . . . your sons and daughters will fall by the sword . . . Your land will be . . . divided up, and you yourself will die in a pagan country. And Israel will certainly go into exile, away from their native land' (Amos 7:16,17).

5. Jonah

Jonah provides a wonderful illustration of the fact that God's purposes of blessing reached out to non-Israelites. The prophet did not like the idea of having to preach to the Assyrians, a people who had long been an enemy of his own people. As a result he disobeyed the commission by which God was sending him to Nineveh—rather than trek overland to Nineveh he went on a boat travelling towards Spain.

Given a second opportunity he eventually got to Nineveh, where he went through the formality of preaching the Lord's message, but apparently without personally identifying himself with it. He went through the city crying out, 'Forty more days and Nineveh will be destroyed.' To his surprise the king and his people sought to obey that message. They believed God and repented before him and, because they did so, the Lord spared Nineveh and its people from the destruction Jonah had been commissioned to announce (Jon. 3:5-10).

Jonah then sulked, because the enemy of his people was not being destroyed in the way his message had threatened and he had expected. He became filled with self-pity and wanted to die. He had to be shown how far he was out of harmony with the purposes of the Lord: 'The LORD said, ". . . Nineveh has more than a hundred and twenty thousand people who cannot tell their right hand from their left . . . Should not I be concerned about that great city?"' (Jon. 4:10-11).

The Lord was concerned for Nineveh, and Jonah should have

been so also. His understanding of the purposes of God excluded the salvation of the Ninevites. The irony is that the book which bears his name teaches precisely the opposite, namely, that the Lord wants to bless and save all his creatures.

The book of Jonah has been called 'the greatest missionary tract ever written'. In a very real sense that is true but, nonetheless, it does not specifically call for the evangelisation of all nations. That call came later with the ministry of Jesus and with the sending out of the apostles for worldwide mission.

Conclusion

The prophets were the Lord's messengers in the Old Testament era. They were forerunners of the apostles, forerunners in mission. As such they are provide effective models for all Christian missionaries.

3
Wisdom as a tool in mission

Throughout the biblical period there were wise teachers or sages in Israel and throughout the Near East. Wisdom was dispensed in Israel by those known as 'the wise'.

Its place in society

Wise sages instructed the young and gave counsel to those who needed it, especially to kings and other leaders. Among the kings Solomon was famous for the wisdom with which God had endowed him—'God gave Solomon wisdom and very great insight . . . greater than the wisdom of all the men of the East . . . Men of all nations came to listen to Solomon's wisdom' (1 Kgs. 4:29-34). Most famous of the visitors was the Queen of Sheba, who clearly thought of herself as one of the wise—a debater who 'came to test him with hard questions' (1 Kgs. 10:1-13).

By the time of Jeremiah and Ezekiel 'the wise' seem to have been accorded a status somewhat like that of priests and prophets. Jeremiah's opponents, for example, claimed that three distinct classes of teacher or counsellor already functioned among them—'the teaching of the law by the priest will not be lost, nor will counsel from the wise, nor the word from the prophets' (Jer. 18:18).

There also seems to have been a general understanding that 'wisdom' was the possession of older people, and perhaps even an identification of the wise with those who served as 'elders'. Job suggested that wisdom was to be found among the aged and that long life brought understanding (Job 12:12). In a passage affirming the opposite opinion to that of Jeremiah's opponents, Ezekiel pictures a calamitous situation, in which the people would obtain no vision from the prophet and when 'the teaching of the law by the priest will be lost, as will the counsel of the elders' (Ezek. 7:26). It is possible, and maybe probable, that Ezekiel used the word 'elders' as a synonym for 'the wise' and that we are to think of the wise as elderly folk with real experience of life and its many vicissitudes.

In the ethos of the Old Testament the sage as teacher and counsellor was regarded as 'father', and the pupils he taught or counselled as his 'sons'. Thus Joseph in Egypt became a counsellor or 'father' to Pharaoh. Joseph's misfortunes were overruled by the sovereign God so that he had a specific mission and was part of God's greater purposes for Israel. He was able to say to his brothers, 'It was not you who sent me here, but God. He made me father to Pharaoh' (Gen. 45:8).

In a somewhat similar way king Hezekiah addressed an assembly of Levites as his sons (2 Chr. 29:11). He, as teacher, was father, and those he taught or counselled were pupils or sons. Solomon thus cast himself in the same father/teacher role as he instructed by means of proverbs. The learner was addressed as 'son'— 'Listen, my son' (Prov. 1:8; 2:1; 3:1,11, etc.).

Its methods

What the sages taught was very largely a matter of practical insight into human life and how it should be lived. They were shrewd observers, who saw in the day-to-day experiences of ordinary people principles that could be formulated to guide others along right paths. They usually expressed these principles in the form of short pithy sayings or proverbs that could be easily remembered by non-literate people. (Such proverbs are also known as adages, maxims or aphorisms.) Sometimes, however, they used longer forms, like a psalm or even a whole book such as Job or Ecclesiastes. Their method is clearly illustrated by one of their number, who describes it in some detail in Proverbs 24:

1. Observation (vv. 30-31)
I went past the field of the sluggard,

past the vineyard of the man who lacks judgment [wisdom);
thorns had come up everywhere,
the ground was covered with weeds,
and the stone wall was in ruins.

2. Reflection or meditation (v. 32)
I applied my heart to what I observed
and learned a lesson from what I saw.

3. Instruction (vv. 33-34)
A little sleep, a little slumber,
a little folding of the hands to rest—
and poverty will come on you like a bandit
and scarcity like an armed man.

What the sage observed he considered (reflected upon), and what he considered he turned into an instruction. The instruction usually took the form of a 'proverb', a short pithy saying that could be easily remembered (ten or twenty rather that a hundred words). Sometimes, however, it took the form of a longer piece of literature conveying an overall instruction, as is the case in the books of Job and Ecclesiastes.

Wisdom material is also found throughout the ancient Near-east and some that occurs in Egyptian and other records has much in common with the Israelite variety. Proverbs 22:17–24:34 provides an example and parallels an Egyptian document known as 'The Instruction of Amen-em-opet'.

As a result of a common method of reflecting on observations of human life it is almost inevitable that the wise of various cultures will come up with similar teachings. The main difference between Old Testament and other wisdom lies in the fact that the former arose within the context of faith in God ('The fear of the Lord is the beginning of wisdom') and under the overall superintendence of his Spirit. It is inspired wisdom and has an important place in God's purposes of revelation and mission. It teaches the proper way to live before God.

Its use in Scripture

Because it picked up what the wise person observed wisdom focussed on things and human habits that were familiar to the hearers. It thus used a thought-bridge that the hearer understood and so made the teaching interesting as well as relevant.

1. In the Books of Moses

Wisdom techniques were frequently used by Moses. It is widely agreed, for example, that the ten commandments are set in a form which closely approximates to that known as *mashal* or proverb. They are pithy and easy to remember, and in the case of the longer ones (numbers 2,3,4,5 and 10) the essential meaning comes out in one simple statement—'You shall not make for yourself an idol'—'You shall not misuse the name of the Lord your God'—'Remember the Sabbath Day by keeping it holy'—'Honour your father and your mother'—'You shall not covet . . . anything that belongs to your neighbour' (Exod. 20:2-17).

The song of Moses (Deut. 32) and his blessing of the tribes (Deut. 33) are permeated with wisdom, and in particular with similes drawn from the author's observation of life:

> He shielded him and cared for him;
>   he guarded him as the apple of his eye,
> like an eagle that stirs up its nest
>   and hovers over its young,
> that spreads its wings to catch them
>   and carries them on its pinions (32:10-11).

About Joseph he said . . .
> In majesty he is like a firstborn bull;
>   his horns are the horns of a wild ox.
> With them he will gore the nations,
>   even those at the ends of the earth (33:17).

In both cases the simile or mini-parable points to a reality familiar to the hearer or reader, who was thus easily able to understand the message.

2. In the prophets

The oracles of the prophets also display the spirit of the wise. Isaiah, for example, has many proverbs, each of which draws a parable from a familiar facet of local life:

> The ox knows his master,
>> the donkey his owner's manger (1:3).

> The bed is too short to stretch out on,
>> the blanket too narrow to wrap around you.
>>> (28:20)

A proverb cited by both Jeremiah and Ezekiel shows how these two prophets were influenced by the sages:

> The fathers have eaten sour grapes,
>> and the children's teeth are set on edge.
>>> (Jer. 31:29; Ezek. 18:2)

Another type of 'wisdom-speak' is the rhetorical question, which is, in effect, a maxim or proverb enshrining within it an observed reality and which is asked in order to lead the listener's mind to an important conclusion. Rhetorical questions often appear in twos or in larger multiples. Jeremiah was a master of this art and was able to use it to great effect, forcing his hearers to see the logic of his arguments. Thus, for example, he asked two questions to stimulate thought and then made his application in the third and fourth lines.

> Does a maiden forget her jewellery,
>> a bride her wedding ornaments?
> Yet my people have forgotten me,
>> days without number.
>>> (Jer. 2:32)

In their minds the hearers would answer no to each question. The application shows them that they are doing something as foolish as a maiden who came to her wedding without her jewellery or her wedding ornaments.

Using different questions and a different observed fact Jeremiah later made a similar application:

> Does the snow of Lebanon
>   ever vanish from its rocky slopes?
> Do its cool waters from distant sources
>   ever cease to flow?
> Yet my people have forgotten me;
>   they burn incense to worthless idols.
>   (Jer. 18:14-15)

Amos also used rhetorical questions and in one passage (3:3-6) piles up seven questions, each of which enshrines a different observed fact. Together they lead to the conclusion of verse 7:

> Surely the Sovereign LORD does nothing
>   without revealing his plan
>   to his servants the prophets.

The prophets used wisdom in order to communicate God's message. They observed life around them, they reflected on what they had observed, and they applied the lessons they discerned as relevant instruction to those they were privileged to teach. Their wisdom methods were integral to their mission and vital to the communication of God's message.

3. In the Psalms
The Psalms are also packed full of wisdom material. The very first one (Psalm 1) is a wisdom psalm which contains a string of proverbial sayings. It begins with a beatitude and continues with similes:

> Blessed is the man,
>   who does not walk in the counsel of the wicked . . .
> He is like a tree planted by streams of water,
>   which yields its fruit in season
> and whose leaf does not wither.
>   Whatever he does prospers (vv. 1,3).

People living in an arid region like much of the Holy Land would understand these images perfectly. They were of the earth, earthy, and communicated most effectively.

Psalms 37 and 73 are longer wisdom psalms which, like the books of Job and Ecclesiastes, tackle specific problems faced by those who sought to serve the Lord. In these psalms the problem is that life was not conforming to the received wisdom of the age. While it was expected that righteous living should bring prosperity and that wickedness should be rewarded by adversity, the opposite was happening—some of the righteous were suffering hardships and some of the wicked were prospering. The answer of both psalms was that in due time, either later in this life or after it, justice would be done and both the righteous and the unrighteous would receive their due deserts.

Psalm 119, the longest of all the psalms, is an acrostic using the letters of the Hebrew alphabet as the first letter of each of the eight verses that make up its 22 stanzas. Every one of the 22 stanzas extols the word, the statutes and the judgments of the Lord and the overall message is that the life acceptable to God is the one that subjects itself to his revealed instruction—

Blessed are they whose ways are blameless,
who walk according to the law of the LORD (v. 1).

What is absolutely clear is that these wisdom techniques played an immensely important role in the communication of divine truth. By working from what they observed around them, prophets as well as sages were able to make the truth and its challenges intelligible to their hearers. As we today might say, 'they were on the wavelength of those to whom they spoke'. In so doing they set a pattern for mission in every age.

4. In the ministry of Jesus

The Lord Jesus was a wisdom teacher and regularly used wisdom methods. On one occasion when referring to himself he said, 'one greater than Solomon is here' (Matt. 12:42; Luke 11:31). Paul says that he [Jesus] was made for us wisdom from God (1 Cor.

1:30). He was, in fact, incarnate wisdom and the supreme wisdom teacher of all time. (His position as the fulfilment of the Old Testament practice of personalising wisdom—Prov. 8 etc.—is a different issue from his use of wisdom and does not come into consideration here.)

Our Lord often taught by means of parables, i.e., stories drawn from life around him and illustrating the truths he wished to communicate. His parables were based on things familiar to his hearers—a sower, a lost sheep, a steward called to render account of his stewardship. He gained an entrance to the minds of his hearers by drawing parallels from life around them. Working from the known to the unknown, he communicated meaningfully with them.

When he gathered his disciples to celebrate passover and institute the Lord's Supper his act of washing their feet was an acted parable to teach an important lesson. He became an observed 'visual aid' to teach the disciples to serve one another:

Now that I, your Lord and Teacher, have washed your feet, you also should wash one another's feet. I have set you an example that you should do as I have done for you (John 13:14,15).

Like the prophets Jesus used questions to make his hearers think about the weakness of their own positions:

Hypocrites! You know how to interpret the appearance of the earth and the sky. How is it that you don't know how to interpret this present time? (Luke 12:56).

On another occasion, when opponents were questioning his authority, he put them on the spot with two questions—'John's baptism—where did it come from? Was it from heaven, or from men?' (Matt. 21:25).

Mark records an instance in which the Lord asked double rehetorical questions: 'Do you bring in a lamp to put it under a bowl or a bed? [in each case the answer expected was no]. Instead,

don't you put it on its stand? [when the answer expected was yes].'
Then followed the application, which would have been readily
understood by his hearers: 'For whatever is hidden is meant to
be disclosed, and whatever is concealed is meant to be brought
out into the open' (Mark 4:21f.).

Another of our Lord's methods of communicating wisdom
was to use proverbs and beatitudes (i.e., proverbs of blessing). The
eight beatitudes at the beginning of the Sermon on the Mount are
a good example. So are sayings like, 'For where your treasure is,
there your heart will be also' (Matt. 6:21) or 'Wherever there is a
carcass, there the vultures will gather' (Matt. 24:28).

5. In the records of the apostles

There is much evidence of wisdom in the speeches and writings
of the apostles. They communicated in terms that their listeners
and readers understood. Addressing Jews they quoted familiar
Old Testament material. For non-Jews they picked up and used
pagan thoughts and practices as the gateway to their minds—the
altar to 'the unknown god' and the citation from a Greek poet in
Athens (Acts 17:23,28). Clear communication was the crucial
issue, and the wisdom method of observing local life was a vital
tool in making it effective.

Conclusion

To be effective, a missionary must enter into the situation of
those he seeks to reach in a way that enables him or her to communicate the truth in a meaningfully way. He needs to observe
and understand local life and to be able to reflect on and use its
wisdom (proverbs etc.) so as to gain attention and cogently teach
gospel truth.

Wisdom is a vital tool for mission. Paul could say, 'We proclaim
him, admonishing and teaching everyone with all wisdom' (Col.
1:28).

4
First-century preparedness

The first century AD is the era of our Lord's life and ministry and of the missionary work of his apostles and their associates. The social, political, economic and religious contexts in which the great Christian events of the century took place were very different from those of Old Testament times.

The changed situation

For much of the previous six centuries Judea, and the other parts of ancient Israel, had been under the control of four major foreign powers. These were:

1. The Babylonians (587–537 BC)
Many Jews were taken into exile in Babylon. The Babylonians also controlled Judea itself.

2. The Persians (539–331 BC)
They conquered Babylon and allowed the exiles to return home. Many did so under Sheshbazzar, Zerubbabel and Ezra. Others remained and centuries later became a very potent influence in Judaism.

3. The Greeks (331–63 BC)
Alexander the Great defeated the Persians and took control of the whole eastern Mediterranean. His generals and their successors in Egypt (the Ptolemies) and Syria (the Seleucids) squabbled over control of Judea. There were periods of independence under the Maccabees and Hasmonaeans.

4. The Romans (63 BC onwards)
Sometimes they allowed a degree of local rule under the Herods, but at other times they installed Roman officers to serve as

procurators under their governor of Syria. The most famous of these is Pontius Pilate.

One result of centuries of war and oppression was that thousands upon thousands of Jews fled to, and settled in, other countries. There were large numbers in Babylon and Egypt, in Arabia and along the North African coast: for example, Simon of Cyrene (Mark 15:21) and the Cyrenians mentioned in Acts 2:10; 6:9; 11:20). There were Jews in Syria and throughout Asia Minor, in many Greek cities and in Rome itself. There were almost certainly Jews in Spain. Because of these settlements Paul could visit Jewish synagogues as he travelled on his missionary journeys, and he could begin his ministry in many places by witnessing first to Jews.

These overseas Jews, known as the Diaspora or Dispersion, quickly multiplied, and it is estimated that in our Lord's day they must have totalled at least four million, one million of whom were in the Alexandria area of Egypt.

The conquest of the East by Alexander the Great in the 320s and 330s BC and his settlement of army veterans throughout the area meant that the Greek language penetrated and was used and understood by people of many races. The Greek-speaking widows in the early Jerusalem church and the seven 'ministers' appointed to divide alms among them are examples. So too is Paul, who was obviously fluent in that language. This highly expressive language was clearly a divinely provided instrument for the spread of the Christian gospel and a preparation for mission.

Traditionalism and Liberalism

Each occupying power had an effect on the culture of the Jews. In some cases, like the Pharisees and the Essenes, it was a reaction of separation from the alien influences and into their own traditions. In the case of the Zealots it involved violence against the Romans and those who supported or worked for them. In others, like the Hellenisers and the Sadducees, it was a matter of trying to make Judaism acceptable to the wider world by incorporating into it elements of the culture of that wider world.

In Judea the Pharisees were the most numerous of the traditionalists. Their name seems to mean 'the separated ones' and to indicate something of a 'holier-than-thou' club made up of people who separated themselves from all (Jews as well as Gentiles) who declined to accept and keep the rules of their club. They developed a system of 'salvation by works' which involved myriads of traditions, i.e., laws of their own making, which Jesus described as a burden too heavy to bear, one which kept men out of the kingdom of God rather then helping them into it. He said, 'Woe to you, teachers of the law and Pharisees, you hypocrites! You shut the kingdom of heaven in men's faces. You yourselves do not enter, nor will you let those enter who are trying to' (Matt. 23:13).

The ethos of traditionalism also found a place in the Diaspora. Here those concerned were known as the Hebraists. When Paul speaks of himself as 'a Hebrew of Hebrews' (Phil. 3:5), he seems to be saying that, as well as being a Pharisee through his training in the school of Gamaliel in Jerusalem, he had been brought up as a Hebraist in his home town of Tarsus.

It seems clear that the burdens imposed by the traditionalists made some Jewish people ready for a message of liberating love such as that of Christ, who could say, 'my yoke is easy and my burden is light' (Matt. 11:30). Little wonder, then, that during his ministry the crowds (including, no doubt, those who felt burdened by Pharisaic traditions) 'listened to him with delight' (Mark 12:37).

Liberalism was represented in Palestine by the Sadducees, who were in the main members of the upper-crust priestly families controlling the temple. They regarded only the books of Moses as inspired Scripture and the rest of the Old Testament as merely a commentary on it. They maintained the Levitical sacrifices but denied the existence of angels and the idea of resurrection.

In the dispersion liberals were known as Hellenists. They spoke Greek and seem to have tried to incorporate elements of Greek philosophy into Judaism. Some of them allegorised the early Old Testament narratives, as Greek philosophers had done with the stories of the Greek gods. They drew moral and spiritual

43

lessons from them, but to some considerable degree seem to have abandoned their historical validity.

Dispersion Jews were responsible for the Septuagint, a translation of the Old Testament into Greek, which seems to have been used by and quoted by some of the writers of the New Testament. Its existence must have helped make some non-Jews aware of God, the Lord, and to some degree open to the gospel. It too was preparation for mission.

Mission among the Jews

There is little evidence of any great missionary zeal among the Jews of Palestine, who seem to have become more and more introverted and exclusivist as the inter-testamental period proceeded. The more traditional rabbis even opposed the admission of Gentiles into Judaism. Others, however, took an opposite view and engaged in ardent proselytising (or bringing those who were 'afar off' near to and into the fold). For them half measures did not satisfy and converts were expected to become full Jews. Our Lord's woe on teachers of the law and Pharisees highlights the position: 'You travel over land and sea to win a single convert [i.e., one proselyte]' (Matt. 23:15).

Before our Lord's time, John Hyrcanus, a descendant of the Maccabees, who had gained Jewish independence in 129 BC, seized Idumea and Samaria and, using force, incorporated the Edomites and other uncircumcised peoples into the Jewish nation through circumcision. In doing so he brought in an Idumean family, the Herods, who in Roman times secured control of Judea and were much disliked by the Jews.

It seems that in the Dispersion a halfway situation was widely accepted, with many Jews seeking to win their Gentile neighbours to faith in God without requiring them to undergo circumcision and become Jews. According to some scholars this was an attempt to put into practice prophetic predictions that the Jews would bring light to the Gentiles and that the Gentiles would turn to the Lord (Isa. 2:1-4 etc.). It was also, apparently, a sincere effort to win pagan people to faith in the one and only true God.

The 'halfway converts' became known as 'God-fearers' and their main duties were to keep the moral principles given to Noah and his family (Genesis 9) and to avoid, above all, idolatry, sexual immorality and murder (cf. the decision of the Jerusalem council recorded in Acts 15:29).

There were therefore two distinct groups of Gentiles who were recognised as entering and belonging to the Jewish community—'God-fearers' and 'proselytes'. The God-fearers included Cornelius and a large number of those in Paul's audience at Antioch in Pisidia (Acts 10:2; 13:43, etc.). The proselytes, some of whom were listening to Peter on the Day of Pentecost (Acts 2:11), seem to have been less numerous. Officially they were full Jews, but sometimes they were not readily accepted as such.

The presence of so many Jews in the Graeco-Roman world contributed to its preparedness for the advent of Christian mission. It made many in that world aware of God, the Lord, and in so doing helped prepare it for another message, which also proclaimed the Lord as the one and only true God.

The influence of Rome

The Jews felt oppressed by the Romans and longed for the coming of the promised Messiah, who would, they believed, restore their independence and reign in Jerusalem on David's throne. However, they misunderstood God's purposes and when our Lord showed that his kingdom was not geographical and not military, but spiritual and moral, they rejected him.

The Roman conquest of the Mediterranean world resulted in greatly improved communications throughout the whole area. There were links by sea with North Africa, Cyprus, Greece and Italy. Roads were developed for military and commercial uses. These routes became highways for the gospel.

In the first century AD Rome brought peace (the *Pax Augusta*—Peace of Augustus) to its vast empire. This was maintained by military might and enabled missionaries and other Christians to travel around freely, at least till the point at which Nero began persecution (in the 60s). Paul, who had been born a Roman citizen, used that privilege on several occasions to the advantage of the gospel and of the mission in which he was engaged (Acts 16:37 etc.).

The multiplicity of important cities, many founded by the Greeks, provided centres of population which the apostles could target and from which the gospel could radiate to other areas. We remember Paphos, Antioch, Lystra, Iconium and Derbe visited on Paul's first missionary journey. We think of Ephesus, Colossae and Laodicea in Asia, of Philippi, Berea and Thessalonica in Macedonia. We remember Athens and Corinth in Achaia. These cities were part of God's preparation for mission.

Roman religion was a hotchpotch. Eastern deities were added to those of Greece and Rome and were given Greek and Latin names. They were often worshipped in a purely formal way because faith in them had been widely subverted by philosophical scepticism. As a result, however, the common people, with a sense of real need for supernatural reality, turned to occultism and Eastern mysticism. Their hunger for reality made some of them ready for the gospel and so prepared for mission.

Morality was in serious decline throughout the Roman world. Divorce was easy and common. Brutality often characterised the treatment of children and slaves. Paul's description in Romans 1 hints at but does not fully describe the realities. There was idolatry. There was sexual impurity and every kind of wickedness. The Roman world was in desperate need of spiritual and moral change and was, unknown to itself, ready for the good news of salvation in Christ.

The first-century situation—non-Jewish as well as Jewish—was in many ways propitious for the gospel. The time had come for God to reveal his Son and to inaugurate his mission of salvation, and in so doing to inaugurate Christian mission.

The mission of John the Baptist

There was another element in the drama of salvation—the birth and the ministry of the appointed forerunner, John the Baptist. His role was to prepare the Jewish people for the coming of the Saviour.

46

John burst into public ministry in the fifteenth year of the emperor Tiberius, around AD 27 (Luke 3:1). His mission had been defined by the angel who announced his birth—he would bring many of the people of Israel back to the Lord and he would go before the Lord as a forerunner to make ready or prepare a people for the Lord (Luke 1:16,17; Matt. 3:3; Luke 3:4-6). As his father Zechariah put it, he would be a prophet of the Most High, one who would go before the Lord to prepare the way for him by giving his people the knowledge of salvation through the forgiveness of their sins (Luke 1:76,77).

In pursuit of this mission John ministered in the Judean desert and along the Jordan valley (Matt. 3:1; Luke 3:3). He majored on personal repentance and the imminent arrival of salvation in the person of the Lord Jesus Christ—'Repent, for the kingdom of heaven is near' (Matt. 3:2).

As John preached, crowds flocked to hear him. When, however, the religious establishment, Pharisees and Sadducees, came to him he literally, as we might say, 'took them apart'—'You brood of vipers! . . .' (Matt. 3:7; Luke. 3:7). Then he told them that they could no longer count on descent from Abraham as the basis of inclusion in the people of God. God could indeed raise up a new people, a new seed of Abraham from the stones! In fact the axe was already laid at the Israelite/Jewish tree. As a nation at the heart of God's saving purposes it was about to be cut down, with anyone who did not produce the fruit of true righteousness being destroyed.

Thus John pointed to a new order in which membership of God's family would be solely dependent on a regenerative act of God, a baptism with or in the Holy Spirit which would make those who come into God's family by faith 'Abraham's seed' (Rom. 4:16-18; Gal. 3:26-28). Jewishness of itself could not and would not assure his hearers of salvation.

Many of those who heard John preach confessed their sins and submitted in repentance to his baptism (Matt. 3:6). Many wondered, indeed, if John was the Christ; but he denied this and proclaimed the coming of one more powerful than himself, one whose sandals he felt unworthy to untie, one who would baptise with the Holy Spirit and with fire (Matt. 3:11-12; Luke 3:16-17).

In due course Jesus appeared and sought to be baptised. John felt unworthy to perform the baptism but with some reluctance agreed to do so. As the Lord emerged from the water John saw what appears to have been a physical manifestation as the Holy Spirit descended like a dove on Jesus. Then a voice from heaven was heard proclaiming, 'This is my Son, whom I love; with him I am well pleased' (Matt. 3:17; cf. Luke 3:22).

Thus began the public ministry of the Lord Jesus and thus was climaxed the ministry of John. His mission was to proclaim the coming of the Lord and to prepare the way for him. This he had done and from that point onwards Jesus was the all-important player. John later said to some of his disciples who had become worried because people were now flocking to Jesus rather than to himself:

> You yourselves can testify that I said, 'I am not the Christ, but am sent ahead of him.' The bride belongs to the bridegroom. The friend who attends the bridegroom waits and listens for him, and is full of joy when he hears the bridegroom's voice. That joy is mine, and it is now complete. He must become greater; I must become less (John 3:28-30).

John had indeed fulfilled his mission. The old order was at an end. Preparations had been completed and the reality had arrived—the King had come. Henceforth faith in Christ would be the vital requirement in relation to personal salvation—those who would believe in the Son would have eternal life and those who failed to do so would not see life and would remain under God's wrath (John 3:36).

When Jesus began to preach, his message confirmed that God's time had arrived. 'Repent', he said, 'for the kingdom of heaven is at hand.' As Paul put it, 'when the time had fully come, God sent his Son' (Gal. 4:4).

5

Jesus, missionary supreme

The Lord Jesus often referred to himself as having been sent by his Father. He was a missionary, the supreme missionary.

In many instances in the Gospels the Greek verb *apostello*, meaning 'to send out', is used to record what he said about himself—for example, 'I must preach the good news . . . because that is why I was sent' (Luke 4:43; cf. Matt. 10:40; 15:24; John 3:17,34; 5:36, etc.). He was affirming that he had been sent out on a mission by his Father, that he was a sent-out one, an apostle or a missionary. The writer to the Epistle to the Hebrews calls him 'the apostle [the missionary] . . . whom we confess' (Heb. 3:1).

The purpose of his mission

The purpose of our Lord's mission is so great, so beyond full comprehension, that it seems to be something of an affront to try to set it out in summary form. Yet, since his mission is basic to ours—'As the Father has sent me, I am sending you' (John 20:21; cf. 17:18)—it seems essential that, if we are rightly to understand the mission God gives to us, we highlight the salient elements in our Lord's own mission. As we do so we must try to discover how he means to send us as he was 'sent'—how his mission is to be the basis of and the pattern for our mission.

1. He was sent to reveal God

In Christ, the Son of God became incarnate—he took our humanity so that we human beings might see and know God in a new and deeper way than was previously possible. God had revealed himself in the world of nature, in history, in direct approaches to and relationships with particular persons, and in the Old Testament

49

Scriptures. But that revelation did not represent all that God purposed to disclose of himself. A fuller revelation came in Christ, who said, 'All things have been committed to me by my Father . . . No one knows the Father, except the Son and those to whom the Son chooses to reveal him' (Matt. 11:27). John says, 'God the only Son . . . has made him [God] known' (John 1:18; cf. 12:44-45 and 2 Cor. 4:6). In him God spoke to the world—he was the very word of God, the prophet or spokesman of God (John 1:1-2,14; Heb. 1:1-2). Clearly he came to reveal God and his purposes of grace to men.

In his life on earth, in his teaching and preaching, in his loving care and his ordinary and his extraordinary deeds, Jesus displayed the character and the power of God and did so to such a degree that he could say, 'Anyone who has seen me has seen the Father' (John 14:9). In him God was indeed revealed. He was properly called 'Immanuel', that is, 'God with us' (Matt.1:23).

How then, we ask, can we, who are mere men and not incarnations of deity, be revealers of God? Is it at all possible that we can fulfil such a role?

Only by passing on to others what he has revealed. We do that by studying his teaching and by communicating his message. We do it by studying his lifestyle and by following his example of compassion towards people in need. We do it by teaching and preaching Christ and by living Christlike lives, by letting the light we have received so shine that men see our good deeds and 'praise [our] Father in heaven' (Matt. 5:16).

2. He was sent to redeem men

Redemption is a major theme throughout Scripture. In the Old Testament God is Israel's redeemer (Isa. 43:1-7; 44:6, etc.). To redeem is to buy back a property, a person or a group of persons that have been under alien control or, in the case of persons, under threat of death. To redeem men is to bring them an effective deliverance, a saving from deprivation or slavery, from death or destruction. In terms of spiritual reality it is to save them from sin and eternal perdition.

At the beginning of his ministry Jesus used words spoken by Isaiah to define the redemptive nature of his mission. He had been anointed to preach good news to the poor, to proclaim freedom to prisoners, and to release the oppressed (Luke 4:18-19). Later on he declared that he had come 'to seek and to save what was lost' (Luke 19:10; cf. John 3:17). He summarised his mission in the sublime words of Mark 10:45—'the Son of Man did not come to be served, but to serve, and to give his life as a ransom for many.' In brief he was sent in order to redeem men. As Paul put it, 'God sent his Son . . . to redeem . . .' (Gal. 4:4-5). And he did just that.

This is not the place to expound the significance of the work of atonement by which our Lord effected our redemption—that is a matter for Biblical and Systematic Theology. It is the place to focus on the fact that the Son of God was sent to take the role of a servant or a slave in order to redeem men. His mission was one of deliverance, aimed at liberating men and women who were afflicted physically, or oppressed emotionally, spiritually or morally, from whatever oppressed them. In fulfilling that mission he sought out individuals in need. He had to go through Samaria because there was a woman there who needed salvation and who would become an evangelist to her own people (John 4). He had to visit the home of Zacchaeus and to eat with him because Zacchaeus needed deliverance from the grip of a greed that made him extortionate in the collection of taxes (Luke 19:1-10).

The Pharisees and others criticised him for welcoming and eating with sinners (Luke 15:2), but he could not be aloof from those he sought to bring to salvation—he went where they were and in a way made himself dependent on them by eating food they provided in their homes. To use a phrase from the Book of Ezekiel, he 'sat where they sat'. He identified himself with them in order to win them.

Can we, like Jesus, be sent out on a redemptive mission? In the first instance we are not the God-man as he was and there are, therefore, aspects of his redemptive mission that we cannot perform. We cannot redeem ourselves or our fellows (Ps. 49:7). We cannot become a ransom for sinners as he did. He completed the work of redemption and ended the need for propitiatory sacrifice.

But we can act in the interests of redemption by seeking, as he did, to persuade men and women and young people, who are living without God and without hope, to heed God's Word and to turn to him in repentance and faith, and then to live by the revelation God has given in Christ and in his written Word. Having ourselves received the truth that God has revealed we can, like the woman of Samaria, pass it on to others. Not only so, but we can follow the example of Jesus in giving ourselves in self-effacing service showing love and compassion to the needy (e.g. Matt. 9:36; 15:32; Mark 1:41; Luke 7:13, etc.), and going out to seek the lost (John 4; Luke 15;19:1-10, etc.). It was Jesus himself who said, 'As the Father has sent me, I am sending you' (John 20:21).

3. He was sent to inaugurate kingdom life

The Magi (wise men) came seeking one who had been 'born king of the Jews' (Matt. 2:2). In the angelic announcement of his birth to Mary, kingship was prominent—'The Lord God will give him the throne of his father David, and he will reign . . . for ever; his kingdom will never end' (Luke 1:32-33). As he began preaching he announced that the kingdom of heaven had arrived (the Greek verb is in the perfect tense, meaning 'has come near', or 'has come to hand', i.e., it has arrived). He, the King, had arrived and in him the messianic kingdom predicted by the prophets in Old Testament times.

The new kingdom was not one of geographical area or political power as the Jews expected, but a kingdom involving the spiritual and moral submission of individuals to the King. It replaced the old order—the law and the prophets had been proclaimed up to the ministry of John the Baptist, and 'Since that time', said Jesus, 'the good news of the kingdom of God is being preached' (Luke 16:16). That kingdom was to be received and entered in the spirit of little children, i.e., with implicit trust (Matt. 18:1-4; Mark 10:15) and through a transforming experience of new birth (John 3:3-8). Those who enter it receive eternal life (John 3:14-18,36). To inaugurate and proclaim this new spiritual kingdom of God was a major element in our Lord's mission.

It should be noted that while our Lord inaugurated kingdom life, several aspects of the kingdom awaited fulfilment:

- The coming of the Holy Spirit at Pentecost
- The gradual growth of the kingdom (Matt. 13:31-35)
- The consummation when the Lord returns (Matt. 25, etc.).

How then, we must ask, are we sent, as he was sent, to inaugurate kingdom life?

Again there are elements of his work which we cannot repeat, but we can and we must proclaim his kingship and affirm that he calls on men and women to submit to his rule. We must plead with them to turn in repentance and faith to him and thus enter his kingdom and receive eternal life. This we can and must do.

To this mission of evangelism he sends us, his servants, as his Father sent him. The great commission given to his disciples and to us is that we are to go into all the world preaching the gospel and making disciples of all nations (Matt. 28:19, etc.).

The goals of his mission

1. Reaching Jews and also Gentiles

In response to the faith of a Roman officer Jesus said that many from the east and the west would sit down with Abraham, Isaac and Jacob in the kingdom of heaven (Matt. 8:11). This was his way of telling the listening Jews that, despite their claim to be Abraham's descendants and, by virtue of that ancestry, entitled to a place in God's kingdom, they would be excluded from it, while believing Gentiles like the centurion would be included (v. 12).

The way in which he contrasted the negative response of his Jewish listeners in Korazin and Bethsaida with what he knew would have happened in Tyre and Sidon (Matt. 11:21-22), and the assertion that it would be more tolerable for Sodom and Gomorrah in the day of judgment (Matt. 10:15; 11:23-24), show that for him salvation was not an exclusively Jewish hope, but one in which other races might benefit.

His insistence that the widow of Zarephath and the leper Naaman received help from Elijah and Elisha, while widows and lepers in Israel were not helped, made the local people furious. Their exclusivism was so strong that they could not accept his assertion that in Old Testament times God's saving purposes had extended outside Israel (Luke 4:24-27).

Later we find Jesus ministering very effectively in Samaria, where many 'believed in him' and testified, 'we know that this man really is the Saviour of the world' (John 4:1-42). In the region of Tyre and Sidon, known also as Phoenicia, he healed the daughter of a woman who begged him to do so (Matt. 15:21-28).

When he had healed the demon-possessed and mentally disturbed man, who called himself Legion, he sent him back to tell what the Lord had done for him to his family in 'the Decapolis' (Mark 5:20). This was an area settled by Greeks and it may be, therefore, that the man and his relatives were Gentiles. When he healed ten lepers a Samaritan was included (Luke 17:11-19).

Clearly, while our Lord's primary sphere of service was among the Jews, his eyes were on a wider world and on the penetration of that world by the gospel. He could and did say, 'I have other sheep that are not of this sheep pen [i.e. not Israelites]. I must bring them also. They too will listen to my voice, and there shall be one flock and one shepherd' (John 10:16). Towards the end of his ministry, when discussing his return and the end of the current age, he said, 'this gospel of the kingdom will be preached in the whole world as a testimony to all nations, and then the end will come' (Matt. 24:14). The purposes of God include, then, the preaching of the gospel around the world: 'the gospel must first be preached to all nations' (Mark 13:10; cf. 14:9).

2. Training missionaries

Our Lord, as the supreme missionary of all time, imposed a missionary obligation on his followers and trained his immediate disciples to be missionaries. In calling those of his disciples who had a background of fishing he said, 'I will make you fishers of men' (Matt. 4:19). He was going to change their work and to equip them to become 'soul-winners'.

We see him doing this:

a) *At Samaria*

As the menfolk of Samaria responded to the testimony of the woman he had met at the well and came out of the town, he told the disciples not to think of harvest as four months hence but to open their eyes and look at the fields—at the approaching crowd—and to see them as 'ripe for harvest' (John 4:35). The disciples were actually in a situation of missionary opportunity but didn't appear to notice it until he drew their attention to it. He was teaching them that wherever they might be, even in a traditionally hostile environment like Samaria, there were needy souls ready for harvesting.

b) *By sending out the twelve*

In a period of busy ministry he was deeply moved by the need of the crowds that flocked to him. He saw them 'like sheep without a shepherd' and urged his disciples to recognise that there too they were in a situation of missionary opportunity, a plenteous harvest. He asked them to pray to the Lord for workers to grasp the opportunity (Matt. 9:36-38). Then he sent them out for a period on mission as the answer to their own prayers (Matt. 10:1ff.).

His instructions about how they should carry out their mission (vv. 5b-15) are recorded in less detail in Mark 6:8-11 and Luke 9:3-5 and clearly related primarily to the immediate task he had given them. The rest of Matthew 10 (vv. 16-42) is possibly, maybe even probably, a collection of our Lord's sayings about mission, which Matthew placed alongside the instructions for this mission. The salient points of the two sections of Matthew 10 will therefore be considered separately.

i) *Instructions specific to the Mission of the Twelve (vv. 1-15)*

- They were to operate under the authority given to them by the Lord (v. 1).

- They are mentioned by name and their responsibilities are defined—outreach to Jews alone (vv. 2-4).

- The message was to be identical with Jesus' own—'the kingdom . . . is near'—it is here now! (vv. 5-8).

- Special powers were to be used and their service was not to be remunerated. They were to travel without money or supplies of food and were to depend on those to whom they went for their keep (vv. 9-10).

- They were to exercise discretion about where they would lodge and were to disassociate themselves from those who would not listen (vv. 11-15).

ii) *Collected sayings on mission (vv. 16-42)*
Verses 16-33 focus on the wisdom and confidence in God that missionaries need in order to cope with opposition and outright persecution. Jesus envisages that those who represent him in mission would encounter negative reactions from society in general, and from their own families in particular, in the same way as he had done (vv. 16-26). In such a situation they are to be like sheep among wolves and, while being shrewd as snakes, must be harmless as doves. They must also conquer their fears by a confident trust in the Lord. No sparrow falls to the ground without him knowing about it, and the very hairs of their own heads are numbered. Since they are worth more than many sparrows they can trust him to know their needs, to care for them in every situation and acknowledge them before his Father in heaven (vv. 26-33).

Verses 34-42 present a challenge to complete commitment. Our Lord warns again of hardships for missionaries and challenges them to put their responsibilities to him above their commitments to the members of their biological or earthly families. What is demanded is self-denying service—taking up the cross, following Christ and being ready to lose one's life for his sake. In doing so the disciple will, in fact, find his true life (v. 39). In such service he is a missionary ambassador of Christ, and those who receive him and his message are by that very fact receiving Christ (v. 40).

Mark and Luke tell us that on their return the twelve reported what they had done to Jesus (Mark 6:30; Luke 9:10). Mark says that he then invited them to join him in a quiet or desert place to 'get some rest'. No doubt they needed rest and our Lord's provision of it reminds today's missionaries that they too need it from time to time.

c) *By sending out the seventy*

This mission is reported in Luke 10:1-16 and involved either seventy or seventy-two disciples. (There is uncertainty as to the exact number because ancient manuscripts support both figures more or less equally.) The instructions largely overlap those relating to the mission of the twelve, but since Luke refers to that mission in the previous chapter (9:1-6), he could not be offering a variant account of the same event here.

What is exceptionally interesting is the way in which Jesus handled the seventy when they returned full of enthusiasm and with an aura of success—'Lord, even the demons submit to us in your name' (10:17). He must have sensed that they were taking glory to themselves and so directed them away from what they had accomplished to the grace of God that had written their names in heaven—'. . . do not rejoice that the spirits submit to you, but rejoice that your names are written in heaven' (10:18-20).

Obligating the church

Between his resurrection and his ascension Jesus commanded his disciples to take up and continue his mission. His commission is recorded with some considerable variation in each of the four Gospels and in the first chapter of the Acts. In each case, however, it obligates the church and its members in every age and in every place. No alternative is offered or suggested. Disciples of the Lord are and must be witnesses to him.

- Go and make disciples of all nations . . . (Matt. 28:18-20).
- Go into all the world and preach the good news to all creation (Mark 16:15).
- . . . and repentance and forgiveness of sins will be preached in his [Christ's] name to all nations, beginning at Jerusalem. You are witnesses of these things . . . you will be my witnesses in Jerusalem, and in all Judea and Samaria, and to the ends of the earth (Luke 24:46-49; Acts 1:8).
- As the Father has sent me, I am sending you (John 20:21-23).

Our Lord made his followers responsible to witness, to evangelise and to make disciples in all nations. The gospel was to break out of the Jewish mould in which God's saving acts had been effected and be offered to men of every race and nation. In Luke's record an indication of the content of the message is spelled out—the preaching of repentance and the forgiveness of sins on the basis of witness to our Lord's death and resurrection.

Some argue that the Great Commission applied only to the first disciples and not to us today. The Lord's promise which is part of the commission and which constitutes the final words of Matthew 28 surely refutes this—'surely I am with you always, to the very end of the age.' His presence and the authority of his person were to energise and authenticate the work of spreading the gospel and of making disciples, not just during the lifetime of those who had been his immediate disciples but 'to the very end of the age'.

In John 20:21-23 and Acts 1:8 the ministry of the Holy Spirit is given prominence. Jesus was saying that missionaries could only fulfil their ministry of calling others to repentance and of communicating the forgiving grace of God if they did so in the fulness and power of the Spirit.

We will return to that very important theme in chapter 14, which deals with the resources available to the missionary.

6

Expansion in the apostolic era

Before his ascension our Lord commanded his disciples to be his witnesses 'in Jerusalem, and in all Judea and Samaria, and to the ends of the earth' (Acts 1:8).

Its geography

The story of Christian expansion in the Acts follows that geographical programme:

- Jerusalem: Acts 2:5 to 8:3 (plus some later incidents—11:1-18; 12:1-25; 15:1-35; 21:17–23:30)
- Judea and Samaria: Acts 8:1-25 (plus Judeans in Jerusalem —5:16)
- To the ends of the earth: Acts 8:26–8:31—including strategic centres in Asia Minor, Greece and Italy, such as Ephesus, Philippi, Corinth, Rome etc.

This expansion seems to have arisen more from divine calling and overruling than from apostolic planning. The apostles and their associates were borne along by forces and circumstances outside their own control. Persecution after the death of Stephen scattered most of the Jerusalem disciples who, wherever they went, 'preached the word' (8:1-4). Thus Philip went to Gaza where he was a missionary to the Ethiopian eunuch (8:26-38). Then the Lord took him to Azotus and into an itinerating ministry that brought him to Caesarea where he appears to have settled permanently (8:39-40; 21:8-9).

Saul, a native of Tarsus and a pupil of Gamaliel, a leading Pharisaic rabbi in Jerusalem, was travelling to Damascus to arrest believers there. On the way he was apprehended by the Lord and in the town was ministered to by Ananias and was gloriously converted. The Christian mission was at work even in Damascus.

At around the same time Peter, guided by a vision, went to Cornelius, a Roman centurion serving in Caesarea. He had the privilege of leading him to faith in Christ and, in the process, of playing a major part in opening the door of faith to Gentiles (10:1–11:18). Next we learn that some of those who had been scattered from Jerusalem by persecution had travelled through Phoenicia and Cyprus telling the message exclusively to Jews (11:19). Some of them, men from Cyprus and Cyrene, who presumably had come to faith in those places, came to Antioch (in NW Syria) and began speaking to Greeks as well as to Jews, with the result that a great number believed (11:21). The gospel was beginning to reach out to all nations and to the ends of the earth.

At this point Barnabas travelled to Antioch to ensure that the church which had come into being there was being established on sound lines (11:22-24). As a result of his ministry there were more converts, and to help in the work of teaching them he went to Tarsus to bring Saul out of seclusion and into active ministry (11:25f.). After a year in which these two worked together in Antioch the Lord called them to a wider ministry in the first missionary journey (13:1-3) which took them to Cyprus (13:4–14:25) and into the heart of what we now call Asia Minor or Turkey. Several churches, which can fairly certainly be identified as those in Galatia to which Paul later wrote, were established (13:13–14:25).

After what is known as the Council of Jerusalem had dealt with the conditions for the admission of Gentiles into full Christian fellowship (15:1-35), Paul and a new companion, Silas, set out on the second missionary journey. They visited the Galatian churches, recruited Timothy into their team and travelled widely in Phrygia and Galatia. However, the Holy Spirit prevented them from preaching in Asia and Bithynia and, through a vision of a man from Macedonia, they were called to bring the gospel to Europe

(16:6-10). Converts were won and churches were established in Philippi, Thessalonica, Berea, Athens and Corinth (16:6–18:18). New fields were being penetrated and helpers like Aquila, Priscilla and Apollos were being recruited.

Paul returned to Caesarea and Antioch (18:20-22) and from there began his third missionary journey, which is less fully reported than the first two. Again he travelled through Phrygia and Galatia to Ephesus, where he remained for a considerable time (19:1-41). After an uproar he left and travelled through Macedonia and Greece before proceeding via Troas to Melitus; from here he sailed back to Caesarea en route to Jerusalem (20:1–21:19). There he was arrested, and after defending himself publicly and before the Sanhedrin he was transferred to Caesarea, where he faced trial before Felix, Festus and King Agrippa (21:17–26:32). Because he had appealed to Caesar he was dispatched to Rome. Arriving there after shipwreck on Malta he was confined under house arrest for two years, during which time 'Boldly and without hindrance he preached the kingdom of God and taught about the Lord Jesus Christ' (28:30-31).

Christian mission had indeed been going into all the world. But what we have recorded in Acts is not the full story, because that book does not tell us where or with what success most of the initial twelve apostles proclaimed the gospel. Tradition has it, for example, that Thomas either reached India or was instrumental in the conversion of people who were the predecessors of the several groups of Syrian and Thomasite (Mar Thoma) Christians which still exist there in modern times.

Its effects

The early expansion of Christianity through the missionary endeavours of the apostles and their associates produced some remarkable results. The gospel was preached in Judea, Samaria and through much of the eastern Mediterranean region. Indeed it is possible, though not provable, that Paul actually took the good news to Spain. As a result of these efforts:

61

1. Individuals were saved

The gospel message was a message of salvation: 'everyone who calls upon the name of the Lord will be saved'—'Believe in the Lord Jesus, and you will be saved' (Acts 2:22; 16:31; cf. Rom. 10:13). In the epistles of the New Testament Christians are described as those 'who are being saved' (1 Cor. 1:18) and as 'those who believe and are saved' (Heb. 10:39).

It was to seek and to save those who are lost that our Lord came, and the task he has entrusted to his missionary servants is so to preach and so to live that men believe in him and by God's grace become 'saved'. And that is precisely what happened in Jerusalem on the Day of Pentecost and again and again in the subsequent days. That is what happened in Samaria and at Gaza as Philip preached Christ. It is what happened at Caesarea and elsewhere through the ministry of Peter. It is what happened across Asia Minor and Greece through the work of Paul and his team. Many individuals became disciples of the Lord Christ, and in the process and through the work of the Holy Spirit they were added to the number of 'the saved'.

2. Churches were formed

In the early days believers, who had been scattered from Jerusalem because of persecution, went to various places in Judea and Samaria and were given pastoral care by Peter and other itinerating apostles (Acts 9:22-43). It seems, however, that they were still regarded as one church—'the church throughout Judea . . . and Samaria' (Acts 9:31).

The first congregation outside Judea and Samaria to be recognised as a church in its own right was in Antioch (Acts 11:26). It was so recognised when Barnabas and Saul became its resident teachers, that is, when there was a responsible and effective oversight or eldership. The next churches of whose formation we have record are those at Lystra, Derbe and Iconium. Here, again, the concept of a local church and, indeed, the word 'church' itself only appear when elders who would exercise a responsible oversight were appointed (Acts 14:23).

Subsequently we meet churches in Asia (Ephesus etc.), in Macedonia (Philippi etc.) and in Achaia (Corinth etc.), which seem to have sprung directly from the work of Paul, though in some cases (Colossae etc.) we have no record of how they were founded. We know that there was a church in Rome to which Paul wrote before he ever arrived there. We also know of churches in Crete where Paul must have been at some point, because he tells Titus that he had 'left' him there to appoint elders in every town (Tit. 1:5).

Missionary expansion clearly produced a considerable number of churches within the 30 or 40 years that followed Pentecost. Again the missionaries and, indeed, other Christians were implementing the Great Commission by gathering converts together in Christian fellowship and forming them into local churches.

3. Opposition and persecution were stimulated

Jesus warned his disciples that they would face persecution—'If they persecuted me, they will persecute you also . . . They will treat you in this way because of my name . . .' (John 15:20f.). Indeed in the Beatitudes, in which he outlined the essentials of the Christian life, he assumed that those who had that lifestyle would suffer persecution—'Blessed are those who are persecuted because of righteousness' (Matt. 5:10).

Again and again in the Acts we read of the local establishment, both Jewish and Gentile, opposing the gospel and deliberately persecuting believers. After healing a crippled man Peter had an opportunity to preach, but the Jewish leaders became alarmed and had him and John imprisoned for a night and warned 'not to speak or teach at all in the name of Jesus' (Acts 4:18). Jewish opposition grew, and soon Stephen was martyred and more intense persecution began—men and women were put into prison and all except the apostles had to leave Jerusalem and flee to various places in Judea and Samaria (Acts 8:1-3). But the persecution contributed to the spread of the gospel—wherever they went they preached the word (Acts 8:4; 11:19).

After his conversion Saul, the arch-persecutor, was himself

treated to persecution—'the Jews conspired to kill him' (Acts 9:23). Later Herod Agrippa, given authority over Judea and Samaria in AD 41, initiated persecution against the church as a means of currying favour with the Jews. James, presumed to be the brother of John and the son of Zebedee, was martyred, and Peter was put into prison from whence he was miraculously delivered (Acts 12).

In the wider world of Paul's missionary journeys persecution continued. Jews from Antioch in Pisidia and from Iconium stirred up a crowd in Lystra and had Paul stoned and left for dead (Acts 14:19). In Philippi the owners of a slave girl from whom a spirit was cast out stirred up mob-feeling and had Paul and Silas flogged and imprisoned (Acts 16:22-23). Then in Thessalonica similar opposition focused on Jason and other brothers, (i.e. believers), and the Christians there sent Paul and Silas off under cover of darkness (Acts 17:5-10). Later Paul wrote telling the Thessalonians that he was boasting to other churches of their perseverance and faith 'in all the persecutions and trials you are enduring' (2 Thess. 1:4). Persecution was clearly an ongoing phenomenon in the life of that church.

On the third missionary journey there was a riot in Ephesus stirred up by silversmiths who were losing trade because Paul and his friends were denying that the idols they manufactured were in any sense gods. Paul wanted to address the mob, but the local disciples prevented him from doing so, and when the uproar ended Paul left and set out for Macedonia (Acts 19:23–20:1). Later still Paul was arrested in Jerusalem and was tried before the Sanhedrin. Because of a plot to kill him the Roman authorities transferred him to Caesarea, where he appeared before Felix, Festus and Agrippa. There he made his appeal to Caesar (Acts 21:27–26:32).

Clearly Luke does not tell the whole story in Acts, for in several biographical passages Paul indicates that he had suffered other indignities. He writes about enduring 'troubles, hardships and distresses', of being in 'beatings, imprisonments and riots'. He says that he had been in prison frequently, been flogged severely and exposed to death again and again. He adds, 'Five times I received from the Jews the forty lashes minus one. Three times I was beaten with rods, once I was stoned . . .' (2 Cor. 6:4,5; 11:23-33).

The First Epistle of Peter reflects the same situation. Peter's readers were suffering 'all kinds of trials' (1:6). This should not have surprised them because in effect they were participating in the sufferings of Christ. They should not, therefore, be ashamed if they have to suffer as Christians, but should praise God that they bear that name (4:12-16). In suffering they should follow the example of non-retaliation and non-recrimination set by Christ (2:19-23) and should simply 'commit themselves to their faithful Creator and continue to do good' (4:19).

John, the apostle and author of the book of Revelation, also suffered persecution. He was imprisoned on the island of Patmos, where he saw himself as a 'companion in suffering' with those to whom he wrote—presumably the members of the seven churches in Asia to which he transmitted the messages from the risen Christ (Rev. 2–3). In those messages or letters he mentioned the hardships of Ephesus, the afflictions of Smyrna, the martyrdom of Antipas at Pergamum and the 'hour of trial' facing Philadelphia and the wider world. Then in his visions he saw a seal opened (the fifth—6:9) and 'saw under the altar the souls of those who had been slain because of the word of God and the testimony they had maintained.' Whatever else the book of Revelation was or is, it was a tract designed to bring encouragement and the sure hope of God's ultimate victory over every persecutor and over all evil to hard pressed believers in Asia. And the implication of that is that the spread of the gospel and the expansion of kingdom life brought about through missionary witness had stimulated persecution for those churches.

There is thus abundant evidence in the New Testament to show that, as the gospel progressed, strong opposition and active persecution were encountered. There was considerable suffering for the sake of Christ and the gospel. And no herald of Christ, no Christian, who in Peter's words continues to do good, who lives a truly righteous life, can expect to be exempt from opposition or, indeed, from more active persecution.

The apostolic mission produced what we might call positive and negative effects. On the positive side souls were saved and churches were formed. On the negative side opposition and persecution were stimulated. But in the overruling sovereignty of God even the negative reactions were turned into positives, as those who were persecuted had new opportunities to spread the good news (e.g. Acts 8:4) and as their sufferings and the way they bore them became part of their witness for the Lord (Rev. 6:9).

7

The personnel of mission

In the book of Acts the apostles are the prominent missionaries. But clearly the work of mission was not restricted to them. Indeed the early church was made up of people who witnessed to the saving power of Christ, and who were used in winning others to faith in him.

The witnessing church

On the Day of Pentecost the crowds were amazed when they heard people from far and wide declaring the wonders of God in their own tongues (Acts 2:11). Peter explained what was happening by quoting the words of Joel—'your sons and daughters will prophesy' (v. 17), and in so doing signalled that speaking for God would no longer be restricted to the few who were specially chosen to serve as prophets, but would become the ministry of every disciple, of the whole church. (A prophet, it will be remembered from our Old Testament studies, was a messenger, an announcer, a spokesperson sent on a mission to deliver a message from his master.)

At the beginning of Acts 8 we learn that following the death of Stephen the church in Jerusalem came under heavy persecution and, as a result, the believers, apart from the Apostles, were scattered abroad (v. 1). Wherever these fugitives who were not apostles went, they 'preached the word' (v. 4). One, Philip, went to Samaria and there saw a considerable response to his preaching (vv. 5ff.). Later we read that some of those persecuted and scattered disciples, who had preached their way through Phoenicia (either Tyre/Sidon region or Cyrene in North Africa or both) and Cyprus, arrived in Antioch, the capital of the Roman province of Syria (Acts 11:19). There a number of Greeks believed and the first church to include Gentiles came into being (11:19-21). Not having been party to the conversion of those who had come to faith in Samaria and Antioch, the apostles deemed it essential to send their representatives Peter and John to Samaria—(8:14), and Barnabas to Antioch (11:22)—in order to confirm the work of God which had taken place.

Before the end of his life Paul got to Rome as a prisoner who had appealed to Caesar. His arrival there was hardly in the form he had anticipated when he wrote his great epistle to the believers in that city (Rom. 1:9-15; 15:22-32). The fact that he wrote that letter to those in Rome who had been called to be saints (1:7) shows that he was not the founder of what was a well-established church (1:8), one which could cope with a detailed and closely reasoned exposition of gospel truth.

There is a tradition, based on an uncertain interpretation, which understands 'Babylon' in 1 Peter 5:13 as a code name for Rome, and which asserts that Peter, like Paul, got to Rome and may have been martyred there. The Roman Catholic church has its own tradition maintaining that Peter worked in Rome as the first bishop there, though not necessarily as the founder of the church. Bishop Stephen Neill says, 'Peter and Paul may have organised the church in Rome. They certainly never founded it' (*History of Christian Missions*, 25).

While we do not know how the gospel came to Rome, the existence of the church there is telling evidence of the effectiveness of the witness of ordinary believers who, for whatever reason, had travelled there. Further evidence of the value of such witness is found in Paul's commendation of the witness of the church in Thessalonica '. . . your faith in God has become known everywhere' (1 Thess. 1:8).

From all this we conclude that every believer was expected to bear a witness for Christ—to be a missionary. There were, and there are, no exemptions—Jesus said, 'you will be my witnesses (Acts 1:8). If we today could, like the early believers, preach the word wherever we go (Acts 8:4) and witness with the same devotion and with the same consistency of life, we would surely be back to first-century blessing!

Full-time missionaries

The apostles—those personally commissioned by the Lord Jesus after his resurrection and including, as a special case, Paul—are the key figures in early church evangelism or mission. They were helped by a band of associates like Barnabas, Silas and Timothy, who are also called apostles. We can, of course, distinguish in thought between the two groups by using a capital 'A' for the twelve and an ordinary 'a' for the helpers.

The apostles and their helpers were not a sacramental hierarchy, as some assert, but men who were given responsibilities additional to those resting on every Christian. They had specific commitments which arose from a divine calling to mission as their full-time work. They also had commitment to one another as members of a missionary team and, because of this, must be distinguished from those responsible for the oversight of local congregations, i.e. pastors/elders and deacons. Sometimes, however, the apostles exercised oversight over a new church and, in the cases of Timothy and Titus in Ephesus and Crete, over churches which were temporarily without adequate oversight, but they were not permanently in that kind of office. If they did become part of the structure of a local church, as seems to have happened in Peter's case (1 Pet. 5:1), they ceased to be missionaries and became elders or pastors in that church.

1. Their call to service

The eleven disciples with whom the book of Acts begins were sent out as apostles by our Lord. He called and commissioned them. In addition several examples of a missionary call are recorded in Acts:

a) *Matthias,* who was nominated to succeed Judas on the basis of the fact that he had been with the Lord. He was then appointed after prayer and the casting of lots, a procedure the meaning of which is not explained (1:15-26).

b) **Barnabas and Saul,** who had already served as ministers in Antioch (11:25f.; 13:1). Barnabas had already served in other roles and so was quite experienced in Christian work. At Antioch there was a direct instruction of the Holy Spirit, received either by the five serving ministers of the church or possibly by the whole church, and followed by prayer and fasting (13:1-3). The two men were then sent forth by the church and, as the record has it, 'by the Holy Spirit' (v. 4).

c) **Silas and Timothy,** who were both sought out and brought into the apostolic team by Paul (15:40; 16:1-4). Silas was among the leaders of the Jerusalem church, which he had already served in a position of trust, and so, like Barnabas, had considerable experience of Christian work and mission (15:22). Timothy had the confidence of his home church at Lystra (16:2) and, from the first letter Paul later wrote to him, we know that prophetic utterances—presumably confirming his integrity and suitability for mission—had been behind his entry into the Christian ministry (1 Tim. 1:18; 4:14).

From these cases two important principles relating to the call to mission arise:

i) The call came to those who were actively serving the Lord where they were—in their own churches. No one should expect a call if he or she has not for a reasonable time been witnessing in his or her home environment and in the service of a home church.

2) The call came with the endorsement of a home church. In every case local believers had a role and the Lord's guidance into mission came along two channels, from God *and* through the local church or its office-bearers. It seems right, therefore, that we today should not expect God's call to mission to come without the confirming ministry of a home church which knows and can commend the person concerned.

2. Their guidance in service

On many occasions the early missionaries were guided by special revelation from God. Thus Philip was taken from fruitful evangelism in Samaria and sent to Gaza at the call of an angel of the Lord (Acts 8:26). After that he was taken away and appeared next at Azotus. Ananias was told in a vision to go around several blocks in Damascus and find Saul of Tarsus (9:1-16). Peter was directed to respond to the call of Cornelius through an unusual vision in which he was invited to eat what for him as a devout Jew were unclean animals (10:19-20). Paul was hindered by the Holy Spirit from preaching in both Asia and Bithynia and, on proceeding to Troas, had a vision which he and his colleagues clearly understood to be the Lord's guidance for an advance into Europe (16:6-10). In each case the missionaries knew that God was guiding them.

But are such revelations of God's will given today? Certainly the Holy Spirit speaks through the Scriptures he himself has inspired. But we always need to be careful lest we attribute to him thoughts and ideas which are purely of our own making. Equally we need to realise that God can speak through visions and dreams, but again we need to be careful, because selfish aspirations and fantasies can be thrown up when we are asleep and can wrongly be taken as guidance. We must surely look for additional confirmation as the Holy Spirit takes up and applies some passage or passages of the Scripture to our hearts and to the issue of a call to service.

The overruling of a person's circumstances was sometimes part of God's guidance. Thus the apostles began preaching in Jerusalem—i.e. just where their circumstances had put them. Things around them, like meeting a cripple at the temple gate or a night in jail (Acts 3:2; 4:3), provided opportunities for witness. Persecution (a circumstance) scattered them and brought new openings (Acts 8:4; 11:19). Opposition sometimes caused Paul and his friends to move on and thus to reach new fields of missionary opportunity (Acts 17:10,14, etc.). When Paul was waiting for colleagues to join him in Athens, the idolatry of the city filled his mind and became part of the Lord's guidance for him to debate and preach there (Acts 17:16ff.).

There can be no doubt that God still guides through a person's circumstances. Health or the dependence of a relative, for example, might indicate that at the particular time God is not calling the person concerned to some far-off place. When he really is calling he changes such a person's circumstances and turns a red light into a green one.

Guidance covers rest as well as work. Paul had at least two 'furloughs' in Antioch (Acts 14:26ff.; 18:11ff.). He had sea journeys and waiting-times, which provided rest. Indefatigable as he was, he did not ignore our Lord's admonition to the twelve, 'Come . . . and get some rest' (Mark 6:31f.).

3. Their training for service

We have already examined how our Lord trained his disciples in mission. In the Acts and Epistles, especially the pastoral ones, we find Paul similarly training missionaries.

The first young man in Paul's team was John Mark, who accompanied him and Barnabas through Cyprus on the first missionary journey. Clearly the training he received did not inculcate in Mark's mind enough commitment and dedication to take him into what we now know as Turkey. He returned to Jerusalem (Acts 13:13), much, it would seem, to the disappointment of Paul (Acts 15:37f.).

The next apprentice missionary was Timothy who, being well commended by two churches, was asked to join Paul and Silas at Lystra for the second missionary journey (Acts 16:1-3). Timothy's training had begun in a godly home where he came to share the faith of his mother and grandmother (2 Tim. 1:5).

It had also come, as we noticed earlier in considering the call to mission, in the context of a home church in which his character and gifts had been recognised and appreciated (Acts 16:2; 1Tim. 4:14).

Further training took place as he journeyed with and learned from the master-missionary. This was effective for, when things went wrong in the church at Ephesus, Paul was able to leave him there to try to put church life on a proper footing again (1 Tim. 1:3ff.).

Timothy had obviously gained the confidence of the apostle, who felt he could trust him to cope with a difficult situation. However, his training was not yet complete for, in the two letters Paul wrote to him, there is a great deal of instruction about how he should conduct himself and about how he should lead the work in Ephesus. Thus Paul trained Timothy by having him with him and by writing letters to him.

We know much less about Titus, but he too had become a travelling companion of Paul and a trainee missionary. In due course he too became a trusted colleague and was left in Crete to 'straighten out what was left unfinished and appoint elders in every town' (Tit. 1:5). His training under Paul was also a success, but again it was not complete and needed further attention through the letter to him which has found a place among the pastoral epistles of the New Testament.

We have even less information about other companions of Paul like Luke, Tychicus, Epaphroditus and Epaphras, but we can be sure that, as they shared his company and the ministry of his team, they too were receiving training. In the case of Apollos, a Jew well-versed in the Old Testament Scriptures and with some basic instruction in the way of the Lord, Paul's friends Aquila and Priscilla received him into their home and there 'explained to him the way of God more adequately' (Acts 18:24-26). The success of their training was soon evident as Apollos went to Corinth where, by virtue of his ability to prove from the Scriptures that Jesus was the Christ, he was a great help to the believers in their public debates, i.e., in their missionary outreach.

Missionaries, then, were not novices but people who had a personal knowledge of the Lord and of the Scriptures, people who, having had some training in Christian work in their home churches, then learned the techniques of mission in the context of living with and travelling with mentors like Paul or Aquila and Priscilla. They had training for mission.

4. Their marital status

Jesus spoke of those who renounce marriage because of the kingdom of heaven but left acceptance of that idea as a matter for the individual conscience—'The one who can accept this should accept it' (Matt. 19:12). He exerted no pressure either way. We know that Peter was married when he accompanied Jesus in Galilee—he had a wife and a mother-in-law (Mark 1:30). Though his wife is not mentioned again in the Gospels or the Acts, it would seem that at some stage she had actually travelled with Peter in his missionary work (1 Cor. 9:5). Since Paul asks if he and Barnabas are the only ones who have to work for a living, it may even be that by her own work Peter's wife contributed to his support (1 Cor. 9:6).

Paul mentions the Lord's brothers, possibly James and Jude, who like Peter and other apostles were accompanied in their work by believing wives, but evidently Paul himself was not married at that time (1 Cor. 7:7). Some scholars think he may have been married earlier in life and was then either widowed or divorced but this is not certain.

The evidence for that view is that marriage was expected of all Jewish males and not least of those involved in teaching the law. Also Paul's reference to casting his vote in favour of imprisoning Christians (Acts 26:10) is taken to mean that before his conversion he had been a member of the Sanhedrin, a position only open to married men. John Murray says, however, that Paul was then too young to have been in the Sanhedrin, and that by saying he cast his vote he merely means that he had supported what was being done.

Aquila and Priscilla were clearly married but, not being full-time missionaries, are perhaps not very significant at this point. More pertinent is Paul's insistence that marriage andabstinence from it are matters of divine gift and, therefore, open to personal decision by Christians (1 Cor. 7:7). Clearly this is a matter in which each individual called to missionary service is free to seek the Lord's will for his or her own life. Whether that means living singly or in a marriage, dedication to the work of mission and to the fulfilment of the Lord's commission is essential.

5. Their relaxation in service

Despite the fact that in one sense missionaries can never be off-duty because their witness is constant and their lives are always under observation, in another sense they need and must have rest and relaxation. The Lord himself prescribed rest for his disciples—'Come with me by yourselves to a quiet place and get some rest' (Mark 6:31). The pressures from the crowd had been so great that they were being deprived of regular meals. As the AV has it, 'they had no leisure so much as to eat', and the Lord saw to it that they got a time of rest and relaxation.

Jesus also affirmed man's need of one day of rest after six days of work—'the sabbath was made for man.' A day of rest to break the pressures of constant work was instituted because man needed such a provision. And God's servants, ministers and missionaries, need that day of rest just as much as anyone else. Indeed in the complicated and fast-moving world of today, Sunday is often the busiest day for those who minister for the Lord, and if such people wish to keep to the biblical pattern they will organise their schedules so that they get a break on at least one full day each week.

Longer periods of rest and refreshment, the forerunners of 'leave' or 'furlough' also have a place in the biblical pattern. Paul had at least two spells back in his home church at Antioch. However, during the first he became deeply involved in tensions then worrying the church (Acts 14:26–15:40) and does not seem to have had much rest. All we know about the second is that he spent 'some time in Antioch' (Acts 18:22f). In addition, he had several long sea journeys and periods both of waiting and of imprisonment which will surely have eased the effects of incessant itineration.

While Paul was indefatigable in the Lord's work, he was hardly an unwise workaholic who failed to organise his life in a way that enabled him to get the relaxation he needed.

6. Their expectation of reward

In a number of our Lord's parables the faithful servant of the Lord is assured of being ultimately rewarded (Matt. 24:45-47; 25:14-30, etc.). More specifically, Jesus promised those who forsake all to serve him and the gospel 'a hundred times as much in this present age . . . and in the age to come, eternal life' (Mark 10:29f). The idea of rewards clearly has the approval of the Lord himself.

Paul taught that all Christians must appear before the judgment seat of Christ so that 'each one may receive what is due to him for the things done while in the body, whether good or bad' (2 Cor. 5:10). Since he is discussing the missionary task of persuading men to be reconciled to God, those who so minister must be included among those who will be so rewarded. In 2 Timothy 4:7-8 the apostle shared with Timothy his own personal hope of being rewarded for faithful service—'I have fought the good fight, I have finished the race, I have kept the faith. Now there is in store for me the crown of righteousness, which the Lord, the righteous Judge, will award to me on that day.'

In the Revelation those martyred for their testimony to Christ were given white robes as they awaited the arrrival of more martyrs and the completion of the multitude who join in worship of God and of the Lamb. They are privileged to serve God before his throne (Rev. 6:9-11; 7:9-17). They are, indeed, presented as enjoying their reward.

Rewards must not be overplayed or regarded as a right we can claim. Jesus said, 'you . . . when you have done everything you were told to do, should say, "We are unworthy servants; we have only done our duty"' (Luke 17:10). We must serve the Lord for his own sake, and never because we think we will gain some benefit in return for our service either in this life or in the life to come.

8
The goals of mission

Before we embark on any serious enterprise it is essential that we know what we are meant to be doing—we need goals!

Mission is surely a serious business, and those who engage in it need clear objectives towards which they direct their endeavours. Our task here is to try to discover from the New Testament what the goals of the early apostolic missionaries were and, through doing so, discover what ought to be the goals of mission today.

The fact that each of the four Gospels concludes with a version of the Great Commission shows that the risen Lord set his disciples, and through them every generation of Christians, a package of missionary goals—'make disciples . . . baptising them . . . and teaching them to obey everything I have commanded you.'

Luke's version of the commission includes an instruction that the disciples stay in Jerusalem till they were clothed with power from on high (Luke 24:46-49). The same author also picks up the themes of commission and empowerment in the opening verses of the Acts of the Apostles, where he records how after his resurrection Jesus told his disciples to wait in Jerusalem till they had received the gift promised to them by the Father and were baptised with the Holy Spirit (Acts 1:5). Then, just prior to his ascension, he told them they would receive power when the Holy Spirit came upon them and would become what they were not yet able to be, witnesses to him (Acts 1:8). A few days later the disciples experienced the things of which the Lord had spoken—'All of them were filled with the Holy Spirit and began to speak in other tongues as the Spirit enabled them' (Acts 2:4). They were empowered by the Spirit and they embarked on mission as witnesses to the Lord.

While the significance of 'other tongues' is disputed—living languages or ecstatic utterances?—there can be no doubt that a miracle of communication had occurred. People who had come to Jerusalem on pilgrimage and who spoke different languages heard the wonders of God in their own tongues (Acts 2:5-11). Witness to the world had begun. The disciples were what Jesus told them they would be, witnesses to him, and the Great Commission had begun to be implemented. It is important to note that this happened in the context of the presence and power of the Holy Spirit. Pentecost made it possible and effective.

In John's Gospel the Commission—'As the Father has sent me, I am sending you'—is followed at once by the Lord breathing on them and saying to them, 'Receive the Holy Spirit' (John 20:21f.). However this is interpreted—as a symbolic act or as a real bestowal of the Spirit—it tells us that mission could only be effective if carried on in the power of and under the control of the Holy Spirit. The promise of the Lord's presence with the disciples as they engaged in mission (Matt. 28:20) in an indirect way involved the Spirit, because it was through him, the Spirit, that the ascended Lord would make himself present at and after Pentecost. John and Matthew thus join with Luke to affirm that the Great Commission and the experience of Pentecost were and always would be inextricably united.

Behind this lies the fact that Jesus himself controlled the outpouring of the Spirit, which Joel had prophesied and which Peter now applied to the Pentecost event. It was in and through the Holy Spirit that the church, initially totally Jewish, multiplied itself:

Then the church throughout Judea, Galilee and Samaria . . . was strengthened; and encouraged [energised] by the Holy Spirit, it grew in numbers, living in the fear of the Lord (Acts 9:31).

As soon as Christian missionary activity was directed to and resulted in the conversion of non-Jews, i.e. Cornelius and those associated with him, the writer of the Acts made it clear that the Holy Spirit was given to them in the same way as had happened in the Jewish context of the day of Pentecost (Acts 10:44). Peter's Jewish companions were amazed to see this happen (Acts 10:45f.) and Peter himself saw it as a repeat of Pentecost—'They have received the Holy Spirit just as we have'—and as a valid basis on which to baptise those concerned (10:47f.). Returning to Jerusalem, Peter explained how he had come to understand this event as fulfilling the Lord's promise about the Holy Spirit in exactly the same way as had happened earlier at Pentecost. His critical audience of Jewish Christians were silenced and forced to acknowledge that God had granted repentance unto life to Gentiles (Acts 11:16-18). Again missionary work was taking place in the energy of the Holy Spirit, whose presence, as we have already seen, is essential to and inextricably bound up with the implementation of the Great Commission.

With this all-important underlying truth in our minds we can now attempt to identify the missionary goals of the New Testament.

To see spiritual life reproduced

It was the Lord Jesus himself who, as he explained the new birth to Nicodemus, said that it is the Spirit, working mysteriously like the wind, that gives spiritual birth (John 3:6ff.). Later he said, as Paul said later on, that it is the Spirit who 'gives life' (John 6:63; 2 Cor. 3:6). Peter told the Christians to whom he wrote his first epistle that they were what they were, 'through the sanctifying work of the Spirit' (1 Pet. 1:2).

This life-giving work of the Spirit effects new birth and turns sinners into saints. It is that which brought spiritual life to those called to mission, and that for which they must work in those to whom they would go.

It is possible to draw a parallel between reproduction in the natural realm and the reproduction of the spiritual life received through new birth. As Adam and Eve and their descendants were to be fruitful and multiply and possessed within themselves an inherent capacity to reproduce, so Christians, as possessors of the Holy Spirit, the giver of spiritual life, are meant to be involved in the reproduction of spiritual life. To see that life reproduced must surely always be a goal towards which they work.

Men become new creatures in Christ and are given spiritual life through receiving and submitting to God's word. As Peter put it, they are 'born again, not of perishable seed, but of imperishable, through the living and enduring word of God' (1 Pet. 1:23). It is by responding to the Word and by calling on the Lord that men are saved (Rom. 10:8-15).

By making Christ known through preaching or proclaiming the word, the missionary plays a special part in a work he cannot accomplish by himself, a work that is the sovereign prerogative of the Holy Spirit. But, because the Holy Spirit uses the word of God, he needs human agents to proclaim it. That is what the missionary is sent to do. The primary goal of his life and work must be to see the Holy Spirit reproduce spiritual life in those to whom he is sent. To this end he himself must be a witness to Christ, a proclaimer of Jesus and the resurrection.

To implement the Great Commission

It must be obvious to any reader of the New Testament that the apostles and those associated with them—indeed ordinary Christians like those who were scattered abroad because of persecution after the martyrdom of Stephen—witnessed to Christ as the natural expression of their new life in him.

Though the Great Commission is not specifically emphasised in the Acts or the Epistles, the apostolic missionaries clearly implemented it. They preached the gospel to all nations, they made and baptised disciples, and they sought to teach those disciples what the Lord himself had taught.

The Great Commission is found in somewhat different forms in each of the four Gospels—Matthew 28:18-20; Mark 16:15-18; Luke 24:45-49 and John 20: 21-23. The Markan version is in a section of the Gospel that is not found in what are generally regarded as the best manuscripts, and so may have been written by someone other than Mark; but, that said, it cannot be dismissed as outside the canon of inspired Scripture. Luke alone records words that indicate the essential content of the good news—'repentance and forgiveness of sins will be preached in his name to all nations [peoples]' (Luke 24:47). In Acts 1:8 Luke indicates how, before his ascension, the Lord re-emphasised the commission in terms of witness for him: 'you will be my witnesses.'

Taking the various versions of the commission together we can focus on three strands of missionary responsibility—three subsidiary goals of mission.

1. Proclaiming the 'good news'

Jesus had risen from the dead. He had conquered sin and death. This was great news! 'Go', he said, 'and proclaim it'—'Go into all the world and preach the good news to all creation' (Mark 16:15). The Greek verb here, *kerusso*, means to herald or proclaim, and not specifically to preach in a modern pulpiteering sense. Those Jesus commissioned were to tell out the good news to all creation so that those who heard it would be brought to faith in him and become his pupils (disciples) or learners. The goal was—and is—to 'make disciples of' or more literally 'to discipilise all nations'.

Luke's mention of what was to be preached (*kerusso* again) puts the focus clearly on personal spiritual salvation: 'repentance and forgiveness of sins will be preached in his name to all nations [peoples]' (Luke 24:47). The same is true of John 20, where the commission is followed by a statement (for many evangelicals a difficult one) about the forgiveness of sins. The goal of mission, indeed of all gospel proclamation, is to bring a message of repentance as the gateway to forgiveness and, therefore, to deliverance from divine condemnation. That is the good news, the gospel, that is to be proclaimed.

As we read through the Acts we discover that the apostles and their associates did what the Lord had commanded. They acted as witnesses to the Lord and proclaimed him and the resurrection (2:29-36; 3:13-16; 4:10-12; 10:39-43; 11:19-21; 13:26-37, etc.).

The same sense of responsibility also permeates the Epistles.

Paul, for example, told the Corinthians of the lengths to which he had gone in order to proclaim the gospel:

I make myself a slave to everyone, to win as many as possible . . . I have become all things to all men so that by all possible means I might save some. I do all this for the sake of the gospel . . .' (1 Cor. 9:19-23).

Writing to the Galatians Paul likened his passionate concern that Christ be formed in his readers to 'the pains of childbirth' (Gal. 4:19). He would leave no stone unturned, he would avoid no personal inconvenience, in order to see his goal of winning men for Christ fulfilled.

Timothy, one of Paul's younger colleagues, when left in Ephesus with a pastoral and administrative role in a church that was in some disarray, was not to forget that he had a primary gospel responsibility—he must 'do the work of an evangelist' (2 Tim. 4:5). He was to be a communicator, a herald of the good news of Jesus the risen and only Saviour of men. Soul-winning though the preaching of the word was to be a goal of Timothy's ministry.

2. Planting churches

The Great Commission did not stop with the winning of converts. The apostles and the missionaries that followed them were to baptise those converts—'baptising them in the name of the Father and of the Son and of the Holy Spirit' (Matt. 28:19).

Baptism is, of course, a personal response to God's grace in salvation—the answer or 'pledge of a good conscience towards God' (1 Pet. 3:21). But it is also ordained by Christ as the means by which a missionary (or a church) can acknowledge that those baptised are Christians. Thus, when Cornelius and his friends came to faith and received the Holy Spirit, Peter knew that they were now in Christ and argued with his fellow Christians that they should be baptised—'Can anyone keep these people from being baptised with water?' (Acts 10:47-48). In so doing he accepted them into the Christian community, a pattern which, as far as we can determine, was the standard practice in New Testament times. In the various Epistles to the churches the constant assumption is that all the believers who belonged to them had been baptised into Christ (1 Cor. 12:13; Gal. 3:27). Whatever else baptism signified, it marked out an individual as accepted into and as belonging to the body of Christ, to the church in its universal sense and in its local expression. Converts were baptised and added to their (the believers') number (Acts 2:41).

The command to baptise means in effect that mission involves what we today call 'church-planting'. Converts are not meant to live in isolation but to be joined together in fellowship and, being blessed with an infinite variety of gifts, to serve one another and together build up the body itself. The first step is to accept them, to initiate them into church life through the ordinance of baptism.

3. Instructing disciples

As reported by Matthew, our Lord's commission went on, 'teaching them to obey everything I have commanded you' (Matt. 28:20a). Converts need to be accepted into the fellowship of a Christian church and then taken on along the path of discipleship. They need instruction in the teachings and commands of Jesus. It is, of course, through acceptance and adoption of our Lord's own teachings that believers mature and become useful instruments in serving him. Timothy was to entrust what he had learned from Paul to reliable men who would be able to teach others (2 Tim. 2:2). The goal was that of establishing a chain of gifted and devoted teachers so that the essentials of the faith would be passed on to new believers in succeeding generations, and so that in every generation there would be those who committed themselves to obey the commands of Christ.

The importance of this goal cannot be overestimated. Christians are followers of, disciples of, or learners at, the feet of Jesus. They are to have the mind of or the attitudes of Christ (Phil. 2:5) and will only do so as they concentrate their minds on him and think themselves into his thoughts and his patterns of behaviour. Christian missionaries must, therefore, instruct converts about Christ and concentrate on his teachings and his commands. They must not put Old Testament commands, important though they are as background to the reality of Christ, in first place. The commission is that the missionary teach them (the new disciples) 'to obey everything I [Jesus] have commanded you.' That is and always must be a goal of mission.

To see God glorified

In the Old Testament the glory of God expressed not just the majesty and the honour of God but his very presence and power. Moses saw something of that glory (Ex. 33:17-23), and Ezekiel in his first vision saw a figure like that of a man which he said was as 'the appearance of the likeness of the glory of the LORD' (Ezek. 1:26,28). It seems as if the glory of the Lord was virtually a manifestation of God himself. At the same time the Old Testament expectation of salvation is presented as a revelation of that glory: 'the glory of the LORD will be revealed' (Isa. 40:5); 'the LORD rises upon you and his glory appears over you' (Isa. 60:2); 'I . . . am about to . . . gather all nations and tongues, and they will come and see my glory' (Isa. 66:18).

The New Testament uses the Greek word *doxa* when it quotes these passages (e.g. Luke 2:30) and on many other occasions. This word primarily refers to a favourable opinion and so focuses on a good reputation, on honour, and sometimes on brightness or splendour. Jesus saw the death of Lazarus as an event that was meant to glorify or honour God (John 11:4). He was deeply anxious that in his suffering his Father would be glorified (John 12:28). He prayed that being glorified by his Father he might glorify the Father (John 17:1,5).

Paul was always concerned that he and his readers should live and work in ways that would enhance the honour of the Lord—'whatever you do, do it all for the glory of God' (1 Cor. 10:31). In many of his epistles he bursts into a doxology, a giving of glory, to God: 'To him be the glory for ever! Amen' (Rom. 11:36); 'to the only wise God be glory for ever' (Rom. 16:27); 'to whom be glory for ever and ever' (Gal. 1:5). Peter, Jude and the writer to the Hebrews maintain the emphasis (Heb. 13:21; 1 Pet. 4:11; Jude 25), as does the book of the Revelation (4:11; 5:12f.; 14:7; 15:4; 19:7, etc.).

This is the pattern every missionary must follow. His supreme goal must be to bring glory to the triune God—the Father who loved him, the Saviour who redeemed him and the Holy Spirit who indwells and works through him.

9

The message of mission

The message committed to the missionaries of New Testament times was the good news of God's saving action in Christ. It is variously called the gospel of God, the gospel of Christ and the gospel of the Lord Jesus.

The English word 'gospel' is derived from Anglo-Saxon 'God-spell' (God story) or 'gode-spell' (good spell or good story). It is what William Tyndale called 'good, mery, glad and ioyfull tydinge . . .' In the New Testament the word is used to translate the Greek, *euangelion*, which, in the usage of the apostolic writers, meant 'good news'.

Some seven centuries before Christ, Isaiah, speaking primarily to Jews who would be exiled to Babylon, looked forward to 'good tidings' being proclaimed to Zion, i.e. to Jerusalem (40:9). Later he sang joyously of those who would bring such tidings: 'How beautiful on the mountains are the feet of those who bring good news . . .' (52:7). When Jesus began his ministry he applied these prophecies to himself and to his mission; he was the preacher of the 'good news' (Luke 4:18-21; 7:22). As Mark puts it, 'Jesus went into Galilee, proclaiming the good news of God'. And the good news he proclaimed was that the time had arrived, the kingdom of God had come near (i.e. had arrived) and the duty of those who heard was to repent and believe the good news (Mark 1:14-15).

Clearly Jesus himself had 'good news' to proclaim. Through much of his ministry this focused on the kingdom of God: he travelled through Galilee 'preaching the good news of the kingdom' (Matt. 4:23; 9:35). In him, God's Messiah-King, the kingdom or rule of God was inaugurated, and those who became his disciples

87

and in their hearts and lives submitted to God's rule became its citizens. That kingdom would progress or grow and be finally consummated at his second coming.

Towards the end of his ministry, when commenting on the extravagance of the woman who anointed his head, our Lord seems to have used the term 'gospel' with a rather wider meaning that anticipated and thereby included his death, resurrection and ascension—'wherever this gospel is preached throughout the world . . .' (Matt. 26:13). Perhaps the opening words of Mark's Gospel put the term in proper perspective: 'The beginning of the gospel about Jesus Christ, the Son of God.' The gospel, the message of mission, is the good news about Jesus Christ and is what everyone engaged in Christian mission is called to proclaim: 'Go into all the world and preach the good news to all creation.'

Its specific content

The specific content of the gospel as it was proclaimed by the New Testament missionaries is to be found embedded in their speeches as recorded in the Acts and in their various writings.

1. The speeches in Acts

Peter at and after Pentecost was concerned to present Jesus, now risen from the dead and ascended to the Father's right hand, as having been exalted by God to be both Lord and Christ. The one the Jews had rejected was in fact divine and was indeed the promised Messiah: 'God has made this Jesus, whom you crucified, both Lord and Christ' (2:36). Not only so, but God has decreed that salvation is to be found only in him: 'there is no other name under heaven given to men by which we must be saved' (4:12).

Philip proclaimed Christ in Samaria (8:5) and then, using Isaiah 53, told the Ethiopian eunuch 'the good news about Jesus' (8:35). Peter explained the good news of peace through Jesus Christ to Cornelius: 'They killed him . . . but God raised him from the dead on the third day . . .' (10:39f.). In the synagogue at

Antioch in Pisidia, Paul followed a very similar pattern to that taken earlier by Peter. He built up his case by surveying Old Testament preparations for Christ's coming and then affirmed the good news that God had fulfilled the promises made to the fathers by raising Jesus from the dead. And because that had now happened forgiveness of sins was proclaimed (13:32-39). Similarly, the resurrection formed the climax of Paul's speech at Athens (17:31).

2. The teachings of the apostles
Reading the New Testament epistles, we get a fuller picture of the message the apostles preached as they engaged in mission.

a) *They affirmed the identity of Jesus as the incarnate Son of* **God**
'He appeared in a body' (1 Tim. 3:16) and was 'in very nature God'; but he 'made himself nothing . . . being made in human likeness . . . being found in appearance as a man' (Phil. 2:6-8). As the writer to the Hebrews says, 'Since the children have flesh and blood, he too shared in their humanity . . .' (Heb. 2:14).

b) *They majored on the substitutionary death of Ch***rist**
Paul wrote of Christ dying for the ungodly and presented God's love for us as shown by the fact that 'While we were still sinners, Christ died for us' (Rom. 5:6,8). He referred to Christ as 'our Passover lamb' that has been sacrificed (1 Cor. 5:7) and affirmed that 'we have redemption through his blood, the forgiveness of sins' (Eph. 1:7; cf. Col. 1:14). As God incarnate dying on the cross for us men, he is the 'one mediator between God and men . . . who gave himself as a ransom for all men'; and it was as a herald of this truth that Paul was appointed an apostle (1 Tim. 2:5-7). Little wonder he could say, 'we preach Christ crucified . . .', and could tell the Corinthians that while he had been with them his resolve had been 'to know nothing . . . except Jesus Christ and him crucified' (1 Cor. 1:23; 2:2). He could tell the Galatians that before their 'very eyes Jesus Christ was clearly portrayed as crucified' (Gal. 3:1).

c) *They emphasised the resurrection and exaltation of Jesus*
God had made him both Lord and Christ. He was now ruling and
interceding as High Priest at the Father's right hand. He had
been raised for our justification (Rom. 4:25) and Paul and his
companions had testified to that fact (1 Cor. 15:15). The confident
message of the apostles was that 'Christ has indeed been raised
from the dead' (1 Cor. 15:20) and now at God's right hand inter-
cedes for his believing people (Rom. 8:26; cf. 1 John 2:1). As one
who possesses eternal life, who lives for ever and has a permanent priesthood, 'he is able to save completely those who come
to God through him . . .' (Heb. 7:24f.).

These great truths constitute the essential content of the missionary message. They make up the good news. The early disciples therefore preached Jesus incarnate, crucified, risen and
exalted and appealed to their hearers to turn to God in repentance
and, believing the gospel, to acknowledge and confess him as LORD
(Rom. 10:9; 1 Cor. 12:3).

The content of the gospel proclamation (the *kerygma* or *euangelion*) is set out in summary form in several passages in Paul's
letters, which merit being set out in full:

I want to remind you of the gospel I preached to you . . . By
this gospel you are saved . . . For what I received I passed on
to you as of first importance: that Christ died for our sins
according to the Scriptures, that he was buried, that he was raised
on the third day according to the Scriptures (1 Cor. 15:1-4).

. . . Christ Jesus: Who, being in very nature God . . . made
himself nothing, taking the very nature of a servant, being
made in human likeness . . . humbled himself and became
obedient to death—even death on a cross! Therefore God
exalted him to the highest place and gave him the name that
is above every name, that at the name of Jesus every knee
should bow . . . and every tongue confess that Jesus Christ is
Lord, to the glory of God the Father (Phil. 2:6-11).

. . . if you confess with your mouth, 'Jesus is Lord', and

believe in your heart that God raised him from the dead, you will be saved. For it is with your heart that you believe and are justified, and it is with your mouth that you confess and are saved (Rom. 10:9f.).

Its inherent power

The gospel is defined as 'the power of God for the salvation of everyone who believes' (Rom. 1:16). Because it is God's word it is an instrument of the Holy Spirit to move those who hear it to obedience. Paul could tell the Thessalonian Christians that the gospel he had preached had come to them 'with power, with the Holy Spirit and with deep conviction' (1 Thess. 1:5). Though Paul, the missionary, was imprisoned and chained, his gospel (i.e. Jesus Christ raised from the dead), which he equated with God's word, was not and indeed could not be chained (2 Tim. 2:8,9). Used by the Holy Spirit the gospel has within itself an inherent power to move and to change men's hearts.

Its unlimited relevance

The gospel is good news for all mankind. It is the power of God to everyone who believes, to Gentiles as much as to Jews (Rom. 1:16; cf. Acts 20:20f.). It is for all races: 'For there is no difference between Jew and Gentile—the same Lord is Lord of all and richly blesses all who call on him' (Rom. 10:12; cf. Gal. 3:28; 6:15). It is for men and women alike—'neither male nor female' (Gal. 3:28; cf. for example, the conversion and the service of women like Lydia, Dorcas, Priscilla and Phoebe). It is for every level of society—the rich and the poor, the slave and the free (Gal. 3:28; Philem. 10-21) and it is to be offered without favouritism towards the rich or discrimination against the poor (Jas. 2:1-13).

In short, the gospel message is addressed to all mankind. It gives expression to God's wish for all men to be saved and to the fact that Christ gave himself as a ransom for all men (1 Tim. 2:4,6; cf. 2 Pet. 3:9b). It urges all men to repent and asserts that 'Everyone who calls on the name of the Lord will be saved' (Rom. 10:13 etc.). There is, of course, an onus on those who hear the gospel to respond by calling on the Lord, asking him to forgive their sins and cleanse and purify their lives and to give them an assured hope of eternal life. The making of such a response is not, however, automatic but rests on and develops out of a parallel convicting and regenerating work of the Holy Spirit.

A solemn duty rests on every missionary, on every Christian indeed, to do all in his or her power to ensure that the word of the gospel is proclaimed to every other human being. That the Lord has commanded us to do this (Mark 16:15) and that God commands all people everywhere to repent (Acts 17:30) leaves us with no option. We must, like the apostolic missionaries, offer Christ to all mankind—Christ's love compels us so to do (cf. 2 Cor. 5:14).

Its social implications

The second half of the twentieth century has produced a strong emphasis on the social side of Christian witness. There is certainly immense social need all around the world and there can be no doubt that there is a Christian responsibility to do all that we can to alleviate poverty, oppression and injustice. But the question we have to ask here is whether or not social amelioration is part of the gospel message. Is it that for which the Lord sends out missionaries?

As we read the New Testament it is crystal clear that the gospel is a message about spiritual regeneration, about the forgiveness of sins, about justification and acceptance by God and about eternal life. The apostles and the missionaries who followed them are not instructed to improve housing or education or medical services or to increase employment and wage-earning potential. They are not told to campaign for or to be involved in the overthrow of governments as some modern 'Liberation Theology' theologians maintain. They are told to preach the gospel and to make disciples. Their goal is to speak and behave in ways that will encourage others to seek the Lord and to follow him as disciples. That, and not social improvement, is what the gospel is about.

There is, however, an obligation resting on all Christians to love their neighbours as they love themselves. As John Stott put it in the 1970s, there is a great command, alongside the great commission. And that command is that those who have become disciples do all they can to care for and to benefit those around them who are in any kind of need. In mission the gospel is the absolute priority; but missionaries, like all other Christians, live under the Christian ethic and they, therefore, also have a social responsibility. It is not that they feed the hungry or educate the children or treat the sick as a means of enticing the beneficiaries into professing Christianity, but that as followers of the Lord Jesus they act compassionately towards needy neighbours wherever they happen to be. If there is inadequate health-care or agricultural know-how, they will express the love of Christ by ministering in these areas. They will always see it as their duty to be 'Good Samaritans'.

Alongside the preaching of the gospel there must always be, then, Christian love expressing itself in philanthropic ways. Sometimes such love will cause the recipients to ask questions that will enable those who give the love to explain that they have been motivated by their Christian principles and then to speak of what the Lord has done for mankind and can do for them. For the missionary, however, the message is not social betterment but Christ as the answer to man's need of forgiveness and eternal life.

Its absolute exclusiveness

In one of his earlier speeches Peter said, 'Salvation is found in no-one else, for there is no other name under heaven given to men by which we must be saved' (Acts 4: 12).

The New Testament never retreats from this. It allows no mixing of the gospel with Jewish traditions. Those who tried to force Gentile converts to adopt the yoke of Jewish traditional law were declared in error by the council held in Jerusalem after Paul's first missionary journey (Acts 15) and in the letter to the Galatians. Writing to the Colossians Paul similarly warned his readers against being swayed by fine-sounding but deceitful arguments of pagan origin: 'See to it that no-one takes you captive through hollow and deceptive philosophy, which depends on human tradition and the basic principles of this world rather than on Christ' (Col. 2:8).

The apostle is asserting that the message of the gospel of Christ is unique and exclusive. It must not be superseded by or mixed with any other message. Paul does not deny others the right to hold their beliefs, but at the same time he never condones idolatry or godless philosophy. He would not accept the idea so common today that people with or without religious faith are simply travelling to God by a different route from Christians. For him there is one and only one gospel, one way of salvation, one message of mission. And that message, that gospel, is absolutely exclusive of all others. It is that 'Christ died for our sins . . . he was buried . . . he was raised on the third day.'

10
The methods of mission

How did the early apostolic missionaries go about proclaiming the good news of Christ? What were their methods, and what abiding principles emerge from those methods?

Essentially the New Testament missionaries were witnesses to Christ—they sought to be what the Lord had said they would be, namely, his witnesses to the ends of the earth (Acts 1:8). In the first instance, those he commissioned as apostles had been chosen to be with him during his ministry—they were eye-witnesses of his life, death and resurrection—and when a successor to Judas was chosen, the candidates qualified by virtue of having accompanied the disciples from the time of John's baptism to the point of our Lord's ascension (Acts 1:21f.). When they spoke in public, they were able to demonstrate that they knew what they were talking about on the ground that they were witnesses of the fact (Acts 2:32; 3:15; 5:32; 10:39). Later Paul, referring to his own conversion, told Agrippa that he had been appointed a witness of what he had seen of the Lord (Acts 26:16).

In the nature of things, those who joined and/or followed the apostles as missionaries were not eyewitnesses of the life, death and resurrection of Jesus, but they were still regarded as witnesses to him. Stephen was one such (Acts 22:20), as was the otherwise unknown Antipas who also had been put to death for the sake of Christ (Rev. 2:13). An unspecified number of saints are mentioned as losing their lives and, in doing so, as bearing testimony or witness to Jesus (Rev. 17:6). Indeed, because so many Christians were killed when the Roman Empire turned to persecution, the Greek word *martyr* (a witness) came to mean a person who had been put to death because of his loyal witness to Christ. From it we get the English word 'martyr'. Clearly, witnessing for Christ was not restricted to the twelve apostles but was the ministry of those associated with and following them in the work of mission.

How then did the New Testament apostles and missionaries carry out their task? How did they witness?

They proclaimed the good news

There is a marked contrast between the 'preaching' recorded in the Acts and the 'teaching' found in the epistles. In Acts every speech except one (Paul's farewell to the elders of the Ephesus church—Acts 20:13-38) is an act of witness, an evangelistic or missionary proclamation addressed to unbelievers. The epistles, however, are letters written to instruct and counsel those who were already believers.

1. Preaching in public

Peter's speeches in Jerusalem seem to have been delivered in the open-air to considerable crowds (Acts 2; 3:11-26). The temple precincts obviously provided an appropriate venue and a ready-made audience. However, his addresses and that of Stephen to the Sanhedrin (Acts 4:1-20; 7:2-53) would, presumably, have been given in a more restricted environment.

When, as they travelled through Asia Minor and Southern Europe, Paul and his companions came to new towns, they usually began by attending Sabbath worship in the local Jewish synagogues and grasping any opportunities for witness there. When the Jews turned against them, as often happened, they went to the Gentiles and seem to have preached in the open air or wherever an opening was afforded them. In Athens, for example, Paul was able to get among the Epicurean and Stoic philosophers and the other curious folk in the market place and to present the gospel to them, apparently also in the open air.

In all these instances the apostolic missionaries went to and preached in places where people were to be found. They went to the people and did not expect the people to come to them. Not only so, but they sought to build bridges of thought between themselves and their audiences. To Jews, proselytes and God-fearers they began with Old Testament history and prophecy, and from what the listeners knew of God's workings and purposes in the past demonstrated that Jesus was the fulfilment—'let all Israel be assured of this: God has made this Jesus, whom you crucified, both Lord and Christ' (Acts 2:14-36; cf. 3:12-26; 7:51-53; 13:16-37). What the Jewish Scriptures looked forward to and anticipated, God had effected through his Son, in turning to whom there is forgiveness and in rejecting whom there is the awful fate of perdition also spoken about by the prophets of old (Acts 13:38-41).

Faced with a non-Jewish audience the apostles adopted a very different approach. At Lystra on the first missionary journey Paul was instrumental in bringing healing to a man who had been lame from birth. The crowd thought Paul and Barnabas were incarnations of their pagan gods, Zeus and Hermes, and had to be restrained from making sacrifices to them. The apostles then preached to them but did not mention the Old Testament at all. Rather they picked up on things in the natural world of which their hearers had experience—the rain, the crops and the joyous experiences of life—and attributed these and the totality of creation to 'the living God' (Acts 14:14-18). Since citing the Old Testament would have provided no point of contact, there was no point in quoting it. Instead they built a bridge to the hearers in terms of the created world that they did know and had experienced.

In Athens Gentile philosophers became interested in Paul and, wanting to find out what he had to say, brought him to the Areopagus and gave him a golden opportunity to preach to them. Again there was no mention of the Old Testament, no survey of Israelite history and no citations from the prophets. Instead Paul picked up on something he had observed in the city—an altar inscribed with the words, 'TO AN UNKNOWN GOD'—and from that built a bridge that enabled him to present the true God, the Lord of heaven and earth (Acts 17:22-31). He then proceeded to declare that God was creator of all and the giver of life to all men. He even backed up his point by citing one of the Athenians' own poets, who said, 'We are his offspring.' Having thus bridged the thought-gap between himself and his hearers Paul was able to proceed and declare that God, the Creator of all, would judge all by one whose authority was proved by his resurrection from the dead:

For he has set a day when he will judge the world with justice by the man he has appointed. He has given proof of this to all men by raising him from the dead (Acts 17:31).

Clearly the approach was always tailored to the audience. The method was to win the attention of the hearers by talking about things they knew and in which they had an interest, and then, when their attention had been grabbed, to present the good news of Jesus and his resurrection.

While the apostolic preaching often produced negative reactions the apostles did not deliberately provoke them. Indeed, they seem not only to have affirmed the gospel with complete confidence but to have respected the persons and the thinking of both Jews and Gentiles even as they showed them the error of their views. They were determined to win rather than to alienate their hearers, and to this end they identified themselves with those they sought to win. As Paul put it when he wrote to the Corinthians:

I make myself a slave to everyone, to win as many as possible. To the Jews I became like a Jew, to win the Jews . . . To those not having the law [Gentiles] I became like one not having the law . . . so as to win those not having the law. To the weak I became weak, to win the weak. I have become all things to all men so that by all possible means I might save some. I do all this for the sake of the gospel . . . (1 Cor. 9:19-23).

2. Preaching to individuals

From the beginning of our Lord's ministry one-to-one witness was an important evangelistic method. When the first disciples were being recruited, Andrew witnessed to Simon Peter and Philip to

Nathanael (John 1:40-49). Jesus himself spoke one-to-one to each of them (vv. 42,47ff.). He dealt similarly with the Samaritan woman (John 4), with the leper and the paralytic (Mark 1:40–2:12) and with many others.

Alongside their public proclamations the apostolic missionaries also engaged in one-to-one witness. Peter and John spoke to a cripple at the gate of the temple (Acts 3:1-10) and Philip did the same with the Ethiopian eunuch (Acts 8:26-38). Similarly Peter witnessed to Cornelius on an individual basis, as did Paul in the case of the jailer at Philippi. In both cases the context was an expectant household, members of which also heeded the message (Acts 10:24-48; 16:16-34). The way in which Ananias went to Saul in the house of Judas in Damascus points to another aspect of one-to-one evangelism—visiting people in their homes.

Paul used this method of evangelism with the jailer at Philippi. When he was farewelling the elders of the Ephesus church he maintained that he had exercised a private as well as a public ministry among them:

I have not hesitated to preach anything that would be helpful to you but have taught you publicly and from house to house. I have declared to both Jews and Greeks that they must turn to God in repentance and have faith in our Lord Jesus (Acts 20:20f.).

Whatever the opportunity—a crowd or a needy individual—the primary method of the New Testament missionaries was proclamation. They declared the 'good news' of Jesus and the resurrection of Jesus who, now ascended and exalted, sits at the right hand of God as Lord and Christ.

They persuaded their hearers

The apostolic missionaries did not merely announce or proclaim the facts of Jesus, basic and vitally important as those facts were. They went on to argue for repentance and faith in the hearers. The facts were not left hanging in the air but were directly and pertinently applied. The proclaimers were also persuaders.

Sometimes, as on the day of Pentecost, preaching produced questions from the audience and gave the missionary a golden opportunity to drive home the implications of the gospel. In a way Peter had it rather easy when the listeners asked, 'Brothers, what shall we do?' (Acts 2:37). The same was true when Philip met the eunuch (Acts 8:34) and when the jailer asked Paul, 'what must I do to be saved? (Acts 16:30).

At other times the missionaries simply moved straight from whatever 'thought-bridge' they had used (Old Testament in the case of Jews, the natural world etc. in the case of Gentiles) to their presentation of Christ and their demand for repentance. Though the record of what the missionaries said is often abbreviated, there was always a step-by-step argument which climaxed in an appeal for conversion. At Pentecost Peter replied to the listeners' question in the form of a command—'Repent and be baptised, every one of you . . .' (Acts 2:38). Speaking to the onlookers after the healing of the lame man he said, 'Repent, then, and turn to God, so that your sins may be wiped out . . .' (Acts 3:19). To the Sanhedrin he said, '. . . there is no other name . . . by which we must be saved' (Acts 4:12). To Cornelius he said, 'everyone who believes in him receives forgiveness of sins through his name' (Acts 10:43).

Similarly Paul told Jewish listeners at Antioch in Pisidia that through Jesus the forgiveness of sins was being proclaimed to them—'Through him everyone who believes is justified . . .' Then he urged them to take care lest they should come to perdition as the prophets had predicted would happen to scoffers (Acts 13:38-41). He told the Philippian jailer to believe on the Lord Jesus in order to be saved (Acts 16:31) and at Athens climaxed his argument by asserting that God commands all people everywhere to repent (Acts 17:30).

Reflecting on his missionary ministry, Paul told the Corinthian church that, because he and his colleagues knew that there was to be a day of judgment which none could escape, they sought 'to persuade men' (2 Cor. 5:11). Thus they were persuaders as well as proclaimers. Having been entrusted with the message of reconciliation they were ambassadors through whom God made his appeal. Their role was to plead with men to enter an experience of reconciliation with God: 'We implore you on Christ's behalf: Be reconciled to God' (2 Cor. 5:20). This complements what Paul told the elders from Ephesus: 'I have declared to both Jews and Greeks that they must turn to God in repentance and have faith in the Lord Jesus' (Acts 20:21).

They taught believers

The Great Commission involved teaching as well as preaching or proclamation—'teaching them to obey everything I have commanded you'. The early missionaries therefore involved themselves in teaching converts. After Pentecost the teachings of the apostles became a focal point in the life of the believers (Acts 2:42) and, when other responsibilities interfered with the apostles' capacity to teach, seven helpers were appointed to free them for prayer and the ministry of the word (Acts 6:2ff.). When converts were won in Samaria and Antioch the Jerusalem church sent representatives to check out the situation and, no doubt, to ensure that the new believers were taught the essentials of the faith (Acts 8:14; 11:22).

The motive for Paul's second missionary journey was to see how the churches of the first journey were doing and to deliver to them the decisions of the Jerusalem council—a teaching responsibility (Acts 15:36; 16:4f.). In their letters, the apostles Paul, Peter, James, John and Jude, together with the writer to the Hebrews, exercised a teaching ministry. They were fulfilling the Great commission by teaching those who had come to faith in Christ.

Of the many diverse gifts which the Lord bestows on his people the ability to teach is quite prominent—'to one . . . the message of wisdom, to another the message of knowledge . . .' (1 Cor. 12:8. Those who impart wisdom and/or knowledge are inevitably teachers and are subsequently called such: 'in the church God has appointed . . . teachers'; 'he . . . gave some to be . . . pastors and teachers' (1 Cor. 12:28; Eph. 4:11; cf. Rom 12:7). This being the case it is not surprising that when Paul wrote to Timothy, who had been left as a missionary in Ephesus, and to Titus in a similar role in Crete, he had much to say about the need to teach the truth. Timothy was to devote himself to teaching and as the Lord's servant was to be 'able to teach' (1 Tim. 4:13; 2 Tim. 2:24). Titus was asked to teach sound doctrine to various groups in the church or churches under his care: the older men, the older women, the younger men and the slaves (Tit. 2:1-15).

NOTE: The younger women were to be taught by the older women, not by Titus himself (Tit. 2:4-5). Paul clearly sought to protect his younger colleague from the sexual attractions which could lead to his downfall if he were to give his attentions to young females—a provision that has abiding importance!

Those chosen to be overseers or elders were to have the ability to teach (1 Tim. 3:2). Timothy was to entrust (or teach) the things he had been taught to men who could teach them to others (2 Tim. 2:2), and Titus was to show integrity in his teaching, that is, he was to practise what he taught and ensure that he could not be condemned for inconsistency (Tit. 2:7). Clearly teaching based on the facts of the life, death and resurrection of Jesus and setting out his commands was a vital part of Christian mission, an activity that went hand-in-hand with the proclamation of the gospel.

They expressed compassion

Our Lord's compassion for people with need is reported again and again in the Gospels. In compassion he touched and healed a leper (Mark 1:41) and did the same for two blind men (Matt. 20:34). He had compassion on the crowds, feeding them, healing their diseases and ministering to their varied needs (Matt. 9:36; 14:14; 15:32). He cared for people and turned his care into action. Ultimately his compassion caused him to lay down his life for his friends (John 10:11; 15:13). He identified himself with us humans and suffered with and for us—he made our burdens his own—for he was filled with compassion.

The apostolic missionaries also expressed much compassion. They too identified themselves with the suffering folk around them. They sometimes healed the sick. They often gave of their earthly wealth to help those facing famine and/or poverty (Acts 2:44f.; 4:32-37; 11:27-30; 1 Cor. 16:1-4; 2 Cor. 8,9). They felt deeply for those who did not know the Lord or the forgiveness he grants and who were on the road to perdition. They were moved by an awareness of the doom of the ungodly; knowing that all must appear before Christ for judgment, they sought to persuade men (2 Cor. 5:10f.).

As Paul said when he wrote to the Thessalonians, he and his companions had been ready not only to share the gospel of God with them but their own lives as well (1 Thess. 2:8). That is compassion, a suffering together with and a sharing of oneself with those one seeks to win. It means becoming 'all things to all men so that by all possible means I might save some' (1 Cor. 9:22).

Proclamation, persuasion, instruction and compassion for those in need, and especially for those without a knowledge of Christ, are the biblical and the abidingly valid methods of mission.

11
The strategy of mission

It is clear that the apostolic missionaries were not their own masters. They were servants of the Lord Christ who conducted their lives and pursued their mission under the control of the Holy Spirit.

It was the Spirit of the Lord who moved Philip from Gaza to Azotus and who confirmed to Peter that he was to go to Cornelius at Caesarea (Acts 8:39; 10:19f.). Barnabas and Saul (later known as Paul) were called to service and sent on their way by the Spirit (Acts 13:1-4). The Spirit later directed Paul and Silas to Troas and through a vision sent them to Macedonia (Acts 16:4-10). Still later the Spirit indicated through Agabus that Paul would be arrested in Jerusalem. Despite the pleas of his friends Paul insisted that it was right for him to proceed, and his friends conceded saying, 'The Lord's will be done' (Acts 21:12-14). They realised that Paul had guidance from above.

At the same time it is clear that the apostles made plans for particular situations and for the wider strategy of mission. The second missionary journey arose out of discussion between Paul and Barnabas about where they would go, and from dissension between them about whether they would take John Mark with them on their proposed second journey. The two separated and Paul made plans to have Silas as his companion (15:40-41). Similarly, when serious opposition to the missionaries arose, they and those around them planned that they move elsewhere (9:23-24; 17:10,14-15; 23:16-18, etc.). Paul himself made plans to visit Rome (Rom. 1:10-15; 15:23-29), Corinth (1 Cor. 16:5-9) and even Spain (Rom. 15:24-28).

Paul also planned and carried out relief missions to Jerusalem

(Rom. 15:26-28; cf. 1 Cor. 16:1-4; Gal. 2:10). When the oversight of the churches in Ephesus and on Crete became somehow defective, he planned careful holding operations involving his younger colleagues Timothy and Titus (1 Tim. 1:3; Tit. 1:5).

Sometimes circumstances such as the opposition which arose in Thessalonica and at Berea (Acts 17:10,14) prevented the implementation of these plans. At other times it was divine constraint in some way made explicit by the Holy Spirit (Acts 16:6-9) which prevented them from being fulfilled. Nonetheless the plans were made, and clearly the missionaries felt it right to think strategically about the work God had given them to do. Equally clearly, strategic planning is a thoroughly biblical procedure, provided the planners, like the apostolic missionaries, remain open to the guidance and correction of the Holy Spirit and use that spiritual weaponry which spiritual work demands (2 Cor. 10:4 etc.).

Basic objectives

The basic objectives governing the strategy of the apostles and their associates were in essence the 'Goals of Mission' already discussed. They sought to see spiritual life reproduced as they implemented the Great Commission. They wanted to proclaim the 'good news', to plant churches and instruct churches and, overarching everything, they wanted to see God glorified.

At the same time there was an obvious endeavour to follow the pattern set out by the Lord just prior to his ascension, to be his 'witnesses in Jerusalem, and in all Judea and Samaria, and to the ends of the earth' (Acts 1:8). This plan was adhered to in a remarkable way in the thirty or so years of apostolic activity. Jerusalem dominates the records of Acts 2 to 7. Persecution flowing from the Jewish reaction to Stephen led to a scattering of the believers, and to witness in the wider area of Judea/Samaria with Jerusalem still appearing occasionally (Acts 8–12). During this second phase the door to wider work was opening as the gospel was taken to Ethiopia, to Phoenicia and Cyprus, and to the

Roman centurion Cornelius. Then from Acts 13 to 28 the witness extends through the Eastern Mediterranean world, from Antioch in Syria to Rome itself. In this period Jerusalem and indeed Syria (Antioch) continue to figure occasionally in the narrative of expansion. Thus the plan, the strategy given to the apostles by the risen Lord was in fact being implemented by them.

Targeting key areas

1. Centres of population
With one or two exceptions (e.g. Philip and the eunuch) the apostles set their sights on important centres of population. They went to towns and cities and, in many cases, to those that would provide a base from which to reach surrounding centres. In most of these places there were dispersed Jews and a synagogue which, as Jews themselves, they were able to enter for Sabbath worship and where in many cases they were given an opportunity to speak. The Jewish settlements thus provided them with their initial contacts and in most cases with some of their key converts.

Barnabas and Saul (Paul) first proclaimed the word in a Jewish synagogue at Salamis in eastern Cyprus (Acts 13:5). When they reached Paphos at the western end of the island their main contact seems to have been with a renegade Jewish sorcerer called Bar-Jesus. Thus at the beginning of the missionary journeys the gospel was taken first to Jews. The same pattern followed in Pisidian Antioch, where initially many of the dispersion Jews responded enthusiastically. However, when Gentiles became interested in the good news, some Jews became jealous and abusive, while many Gentiles became believers (Acts 13:14-48). We don't know how long the apostles remained in the city, but there is a significant comment in the very next verse: 'The word of the Lord spread through the whole region' (v. 49). Clearly Antioch in Pisidia was a key centre of population from which the gospel radiated to other places.

Paul spent a considerable time in Ephesus and, while he was there, Jews and Greeks from other parts of the Roman province of Asia 'heard the word of the Lord' (Acts 19:10). It is widely believed that the church at Colossae came into being at this time, possibly through the work of Epaphras, who himself belonged to the town or at least to the church established there (Col. 1:7; 4:12). We have no record of Paul actually visiting Colossae, though when he wrote to Philemon he expressed a desire to do so (Phm. 22). The Laodicean church to which Paul also wrote a letter—one that has not survived (Col. 4:16)—is thought to have had a similar origin.

The longer-term result of Paul's time in Ephesus, and no doubt of the work of others, was a cluster of seven churches to which the risen Christ sent very specific messages through John, then a prisoner in Patmos (Rev. 2 and 3). Strategically the targeting of Ephesus, the chief city of an important Roman province, was of great value in the furtherance of mission.

2. Areas where Christ was not known
Paul regarded himself as having special responsibility to take the gospel to those who had not as yet heard of Christ. In pursuit of this goal he was anxious not to build on foundations others had laid and presumably, therefore, not to appear to be taking credit for their work.

It has always been my ambition to preach the gospel where Christ was not known, so that I would not be building on someone else's foundation . . . This is why I have often been hindered from coming to you (Rom. 15:20-22).

Though Paul was keen to visit and to preach the gospel in Rome—'that I might have a harvest among you, just as I have had among the other Gentiles' (Rom. 1:13-15)—his priority was to preach in areas that were totally unevangelised. With this in view he had covered a huge arc of land from Jerusalem to Illyricum, i.e. from Palestine to the Adriatic. Now feeling that there was no more place for him in these regions his mind had turned to Spain, another new field, and his hope was to visit Rome as he travelled there (Rom. 15:19,23,24). In the event things worked out differently and he got to Rome not as a free agent but as a prisoner waiting to make his appeal to Caesar (Acts 28).

Sensible tactics

The apostolic missionaries exercised a great deal of sound common sense. They were totally dedicated to the task of mission and sought to win rather than antagonise people. Though they were prepared to suffer or die for the gospel they did not court martyrdom and were careful to protect their own lives as far as was possible. Examination of their tactics throws up several important principles:

1. Concentrating on the receptive

When the Lord sent the twelve out on mission he told them that, when they found anyone who would not welcome them or listen to their words, they should shake the dust off their feet as they left that home or that town (Matt.10:14). He was simply saying that they should not waste valuable time or energy or confrontational argument on unreceptive people. By implication he was encouraging them to concentrate on the receptive. In doing this he was not, as the following verses show, suggesting that in their missionary work they would be able to avoid opposition—they would be 'like sheep among wolves' and would discover that even close relatives could turn against them (Matt. 10:16-36).

The early witness in Jerusalem and Judea was directed solely to Jewish people, many of whom were enthusiastically receptive to the word. A receptive three thousand accepted it at Pentecost. The opposition that soon arose was orchestrated by the religious leaders, whose antagonism towards the gospel did not, however, stop many more receptive folk from becoming believers (Acts 4:4; 6:1).

Philip's ministry in Samaria was among people who had some knowledge of God—who were 'half-Israelite and half-Gentile'. At Gaza an Ethiopian eunuch who was in a very real sense a 'God-fearer' was converted (Acts 8:26-39). Soon Peter led to faith Cornelius, a Roman officer who with his family (or household) was also 'God-fearing' (Acts 10). In each case the gospel was being proclaimed to people who were in a receptive state of mind.

Later on, as Paul carried out his missionary work, he felt himself obliged to offer the gospel first to his fellow Jews (Acts 13:46 etc.; Rom. 1:16b). This was good sense because the Jews, even in dispersion, had a knowledge of God, and so had common elements of belief with the missionaries which enabled each party to understand and communicate with the other fairly easily. Equally important was the fact that when Paul and his colleagues arrived in a new centre the local Jews were initially curious and prepared to listen to what the missionaries had to say. They were to a degree receptive both to the message and to the messengers.

While Paul usually began by evangelising Jews, some of whom turned to Christ, he often found that as communities they quickly became antagonistic. He then turned to Gentiles who, like the Jews, were initially receptive (Acts 13:46,48, etc.) but who sometimes also changed and became opposed to the gospel and to the missionaries (Acts 16:19; 17:5-9,13-15; 19:23–20:1). When that happened, Paul and his friends usually moved away fairly quickly (Acts 14:20; 16:40; 17:10,14, etc.).

Clearly, then, the apostolic missionaries did not endlessly pursue people who were obdurate or antagonistic. They did not allow themselves to be trapped in a situation where their ministrations could not have been effective but would rather have increased the antagonism against the gospel. Instead they moved on to other people and to new fields. It seems as if their concern for the success of the gospel drove them to seek out and witness to people who were receptive, whose hearts, like that of Lydia at Philippi, the Lord was opening.

2. Wise approaches and withdrawals
We have already noticed how the apostles made their initial contacts with Jews who shared with them the background of the Old

Testament and, indeed, since they were Jews themselves, of contemporary Judaism. That they won converts who were Jews shows that this was a wise approach.

While Paul waited for his colleagues to arrive in Athens he was able to reason with the local Jews and God-fearing Greeks in their synagogue and with whoever happened to be in the market place (Acts 17:17). Out of this came a unique opportunity to witness to the philosophers at the Areopagus. His approach was through something they knew—their altar to the 'unknown god'—and with no reference at all to the Old Testament which would not have been known to that audience. Earlier he had made a similar response at Lystra to non-Jewish people who thought he was a god (Acts 14:14-18).

In times of emergency he wisely withdrew from confrontational situations that threatened his life and the witness to the gospel. As a new disciple he had been let out of Damascus in a basket slung over or through a hole in the wall (Acts 9:25). He and his team were always ready to shake the dust off their feet against the wanton (Acts 13:51; 17:10,14; 18:6) and to move on to new spheres of opportunity.

At the same time Paul made wise use of his Roman citizenship, which was a kind of trump card that ensured relief when Roman officials mistreated him (Acts 16:37; 22:25-29). Equally wisely he lost no time in taking action to save his life when, through his nephew, he received a report of a plot to kill him (Acts 23:16-35). Clearly the apostles did not think that the Lord wanted them to risk their lives unnecessarily; they were wise in taking such action as was necessary to maintain personal safety.

3. Maintaining team and church fellowship

Paul's letters abound in tender references to his colleagues and to the churches to which he ministered. His letters normally began with a warm greeting to the recipients. They shared information about the Lord's work, and many of them ended with a series of greetings and messages for individuals (e.g. Eph. 6:21-22; Phil. 4:21-22; Col. 4:10-18). The same is true of the general epistles (e.g. Heb. 13:24; 1 Pet. 5:13,14; 3 John 14, etc.).

Prayer letters are not a twentieth-century invention but a thoroughly biblical means of maintaining fellowship among missionaries and the churches that send or support them.

Clearly the missionaries of the New Testament era were not individualists who did 'their own thing' without thought of their fellow workers or fellowship with supporting churches. They knew themselves to be interrelated as members of God's missionary army. As Paul wrote, 'The man who plants and the man who waters have one purpose . . . we are God's fellow-workers' (1 Cor. 3:8-9).

On the broader canvas of church life, in which mission is firmly set, the analogy which is often drawn between the human body and the church or body of Christ is absolutely relevant:

> Just as each of us has one body with many members and these members do not all have the same function, so in Christ we who are many form one body, and each member belongs to all the others (Rom. 12:4,5).

> The body is a unit, though it is made up of many parts; and though all its parts are many, they form one body. So it is with Christ. For we were all baptised by one Spirit into one body . . . Now you are the body of Christ, and each one of you is a part of it. And in the church [the body of Christ] God has appointed first of all apostles [essentially missionaries], second prophets . . . ' (1 Cor. 12:12-30).

Isolationism is not and cannot be an option in Christian mission. Each worker has particular gifts that should be integrated with the gifts of others, so that the body can function to its optimum capacity. Any sound strategy of or for mission must so plan the location and work of individuals that they make their maximum contribution to the overall effort. Team and church fellowship are essentials of good strategy.

12
The Holy Spirit in mission

As the third person of the divine trinity, the Holy Spirit shares divine omnipotence. He is *power*, the very power of God.

We must never think, however, of the Holy Spirit as merely an invisible divine force or influence. He is, of course, invisible like the wind, recognised only by the effects of his presence (John 3:8). When *he* is present in power, things happen. Thus our Lord was able to assure his disciples that, when in the course of their work for him they would be arrested and interrogated, they would be able to rely on the Spirit of God to speak within them and to give them words appropriate to their situation (Matt. 10:19-20; Mark 13:11).

Just before his crucifixion Jesus told the disciples that after his departure from them they would have the privilege of another comforter (counsellor/strengthener), the Holy Spirit, who would bear witness to himself in tandem with their own witness to him (John 15:26). In doing so he, the Spirit, and not the disciples themselves, would convict the world of sin, of righteousness and of judgment (John 16:8). In a word, he would make a life-changing impact on those to whom witness was addressed.

After his resurrection and before his ascension we find Jesus commissioning his disciples—'As the Father has sent me, I am sending you' (John 20:21). To ensure that they realised that they could not win men to God and to right living by their own efforts he 'breathed on them and said, "Receive the Holy Spirit."' He then put the focus on the heart of evangelistic or missionary work, namely, the bringing of forgiveness to sinners (John 20:23). Whatever else this passage teaches, it emphasises the fact that a ministry that brings men and women to forgiveness is a ministry carried out in the power of the Holy Spirit. Without his presence and activity no one could or would be forgiven. He testifies to Christ, he discloses Christ, he brings glory to Christ and he empowers the disciples of Christ for witness—they receive power and they become witnesses (Acts 1:8). His is the power, the real and only effective power for mission.

His power in the mission of Jesus

It is only with awe and bated breath that we dare even mention the relation between God the Son and God the Spirit. Here indeed, is deep mystery beyond our ken.

Yet God has seen fit to reveal the fact that the Holy Spirit came upon Jesus in a special way at his baptism in the Jordan (Matt. 3:16 etc.). Matthew and Luke each tell us that immediately after this the Spirit led Jesus into the wilderness to be tempted by Satan. Luke says he was 'full of the Holy Spirit', an expression which above all else means that he was controlled by the Spirit (Luke 4:1). Luke also tells us that when he returned to Galilee he went into the synagogue at Nazareth and read publicly from Isaiah, asserting that the words 'The Spirit of the Lord is on me' were, in fact, being fulfilled there and then in himself. He was claiming to be the Messiah, the one whose mission was to preach good news, and whose authority and power to do so came from an enduement or anointing by the Holy Spirit (Luke 4:16-21).

The role the Spirit took in the initiation of our Lord's ministry obviously continued throughout that ministry, even if the fact is not spelled out at every point. One clear reference occurs in the record of the occasion when he was accused of casting out demons by Beelzebub, the prince of demons. His reply was a clear assertion that he had acted under the control of and in the power of the Spirit: 'if I drive out demons by the Spirit of God, then the kingdom of God has come upon you' (Matt. 12:28). Again, when the mission of the seventy was completed and the missioners came back full of joy, Jesus himself was 'full of joy through the Holy Spirit' (Luke 10:21).

114

Years later, Peter, who had firsthand knowledge of our Lord's ministry, was able to tell Cornelius that God had anointed Jesus of Nazareth with the Holy Spirit and power and that it was as one so anointed that he 'went around doing good and healing all who were under the power of the devil, because God was with him' (Acts 10:38).

Clearly, then, Jesus carried on his mission under the control of and in the power of the Holy Spirit.

His power in the work of the apostles

Immediately before his ascension the risen Lord renewed his promises about the coming of the Holy Spirit and made them directly applicable to the mission to which he had commissioned the disciples: 'you will receive power when the Holy Spirit comes on you; and you will be my witnesses . . .' (Acts 1:8). For the disciples to receive the Spirit was to receive power, power for mission. Those who receive him become witnesses, and it is not for one moment envisaged that they should be anything other than or anything less than witnesses.

The fulfilment of these promises came on the Day of Pentecost when the Holy Spirit came upon and filled or took control of each of the disciples. The result was that they began to speak in tongues (or languages) other than their own. This they did as the Spirit enabled them, as he gave them utterance. He was the power in their lives, power to witness, power that turned timid Galilean disciples into bold and effective heralds of the gospel.

Soon after this the apostles were in trouble with the Jerusalem authorities. Peter and John were arrested and, as Luke tells us, Peter, being filled with the Holy Spirit (Acts 4:8), vigorously defended their missionary activities. He was, in effect, experiencing a fulfilment of Jesus' promise that when arrested the Spirit would give the disciples words appropriate to their need at the time. On their release the two disciples joined with others in fervent prayer. Then followed a new filling of the Spirit, a new manifestation of his control in their lives. Again there was power for witness, for

115

mission: 'they spoke the word of God boldly' (Acts 4:31).

Those appointed to minister to the material needs of widows (Acts 6:1-6) were chosen on the basis that they were known to be full of the Holy Spirit and wisdom—they were men who lived under the control of the Spirit. And so it went on—the Spirit took hold of Philip (Acts 8:39). He guided Peter to go with the ambassadors sent by Cornelius, and he acted sovereignly as Peter preached to bring Cornelius and others into the family of the saved (Acts 10:19,44-46; 11:12). He called Barnabas and Saul into mission (Acts 13:1-4) and he guided Paul and the others as to where they should go on their missionary journeys (Acts 16:6,7).

When difficulty arose over the position of non-Jewish or Gentile converts in the church fellowship, the apostles at Jerusalem were joined by Barnabas and Paul and other representatives of the Antioch church. The consultation resulted in an agreed statement which was sent to Antioch, saying that the decision being communicated was one in which the Holy Spirit had had a primary role: 'It seemed good to the Holy Spirit and to us . . .' (Acts 15:28).

In many of these instances the Spirit worked inwardly in the hearts and minds of God's people, thus ensuring that God's will was done. In one sense he worked in tandem with the disciples, but in another he acted sovereignly to achieve the will of God. His work was never stereotyped; was always invisible and mysterious, yet exciting and known by its effects as lives were changed and as disciples were borne along and guided in what they did and said.

The writings of the apostles make it abundantly clear that no one can become or be a Christian apart from an inward regenerating work of the Holy Spirit. Thus, if converts are to be won from unbelief to faith in Christ, there must be a work of the Holy Spirit. Jesus had said that apart from such a work no one could enter the kingdom of God. He went on to say that while in normal or natural reproduction the flesh produces flesh, it is the Spirit, and the Spirit alone, who gives birth to spirit, i.e. to spiritual life (John 3:5-7). Evangelism/mission thus depends totally on this inward regenerating work of the Holy Spirit.

The apostles developed and reiterated this basic truth. For them, as for the Lord Jesus, spiritual rebirth is the result of a mysterious working of the Holy Spirit. It is he who renews and regenerates; it is he who is poured out on us generously through Jesus Christ our Saviour (Tit. 3:5-6). It is he who brings cleansing sanctification and justification to the repentant sinner (1 Cor. 6:11). It is he who makes the regenerate believer aware that he has become a son of God—he 'testifies with our spirit that we are God's children' (Rom. 8:15-17). The full reality of this is that the Holy Spirit lives in the believer's heart and makes his relationship as a son/child of God meaningful and precious—'God sent the Spirit of his Son into our hearts, the Spirit who calls out, "Abba, Father."' (Gal. 4:6). Because the Holy Spirit dwells with the believer he is able to address God in the most intimate way—just as a trusting infant would address a loving father as "Papa" or "Daddy". Little wonder Paul can say, 'if anyone does not have the Spirit of Christ, he does not belong to Christ' (Rom. 8:9).

Writing to the Corinthians Paul insisted that he and his fellow missionaries were absolutely dependent on the Holy Spirit. They spoke words which they had been taught by the Holy Spirit (1 Cor. 2:13). And they recognised that such words were only understood and followed by those who had the Spirit—'The man without the Spirit does not accept the things that come from the Spirit of God . . . he cannot understand them, because they are spiritually discerned' (1 Cor. 2:14).

Clearly, then, the penetration of human hearts by divine truth depends on a twofold working of the Holy Spirit. He works to teach those who witness to Jesus what they should say, thus fulfilling our Lord's promises recorded in John 16:12-15. And he also works to open the hearts and minds of those who receive the witness to Jesus. He convicts or brings people to a state of assured conviction about the realities of sin, righteousness and judgment (John 16:8-11). It is he and he alone who brings men and women to the point where they can with integrity say 'Jesus is Lord' (1 Cor. 12:3). In his second letter to Corinth Paul puts these basic truths in different words. He says that the Spirit gives life (3:6); that he ministers righteousness—he produces good behaviour (3:8-9); and that he brings freedom—'where the Spirit of the Lord is, there is freedom' (3:17).

Then there is the fact that the Spirit bestowed gifts on believers and did so with a view to evangelism and to the upbuilding of church life (Rom. 12:6-8; 1 Cor. 12:4-11; Eph. 4:7-13). Gifts are not given to boost a believer's personal ego but 'for the common good', that is, for the benefit of the believing community (1 Cor. 12:7). Their purpose is the equipping of the people of God for works of service, works that include evangelism and teaching, works that are at the very heart of the great commission—of mission.

Like their Lord before them, the apostles carried on their mission under the control of and in the power of the Holy Spirit. They acknowledged that without his presence and secret workings conversions would not occur; or, to put it another way, mission would fail.

His power in mission today

Mission is for all believers. None can escape from our Lord's commission, 'Make disciples . . . you will be witnesses unto me . . .'

Whether the Lord calls us to some faraway place or just sends us to a nearby street and to a particular house, as happened to Ananias (Acts 9:11), is beside the point. Each of us has a mission from the Lord, a mission that involves witness and that needs power beyond anything we ourselves possess. What matters is that we, like the Lord Jesus and like his apostles, fulfil the commission under the control of and in the power of the Holy Spirit.

But we cannot, and indeed must not, attempt to manipulate God's Holy Spirit. It is not even for us to assert that he is actually filling or controlling our lives, for in Scripture it was always an observer who noticed such fullness, such control.

However, Scripture does give us guidance. Two things seem absolutely predominant.

1. The Power of the Spirit is experienced in union with Christ
Paul's great phrase to define the believer's relationship to the Lord
is 'in Christ'. Theologians sometimes speak of this as 'faith-
union'. The meaning is that faith, which reaches out from the believing soul and into Christ, creates a living bond, a union of life, without which mission and much else besides can never be effective.

Jesus pictured himself as a vine and his disciples as his bran-
ches and stressed that no branch, no disciple, could bear fruit unless
he was in a living union with himself—'. . . apart from me you
can do nothing' (John 15:1-5).

And when he left the earthly tabernacle of his physical body
the disciples were told to wait in Jerusalem till they would be clothed
with power from on high (Luke 24:49). They had a missionary commission, but they could not, they dare not, begin to fulfil it until
the Spirit came into their lives to establish union with the Lord
and to empower them for service. At Pentecost he, the Holy
Spirit, came to dwell in their hearts and to energise their service. And as we have seen, he did just that.

Later on Paul put this truth in different words—'we were all
(i.e. all believers) baptised by one Spirit into one body—whether
Jews or Greeks, slave or free—and we were all given the one
Spirit to drink' (1 Cor. 12:13). By a work of the Holy Spirit believers are brought into the body of Christ and thereafter they are 'in
Christ'. They are united to him by faith and are members of that
body he identifies as specially his own, namely the church.

This union between believing men and the Lord is indeed our
supreme privilege. It is the essential basis of all true Christian
mission.

2. The power of the Holy Spirit is experienced in answer to prayer
Spiritual victories are won on our knees. In mission we are not
battling with physical forces, not even with the men and women
we seek to win. We are battling against hidden forces of evil
that have taken hold of God's creatures and that only he can
conquer. How good to know that the battle is not ours but the Lord's!
Yet we are involved. We are called to mission and to prayer for

119

success in mission. Our Lord's words in answer to disciples troubled by their inability to cast out a demon are true of all mission—'This kind can come out only by prayer' (Mark 9:29).

Again and again in Scripture advance in mission followed earnest and persistent prayer. After the ascension, as they awaited Pentecost, the disciples 'all joined together constantly in prayer' (Acts 1:14). In times of opposition they prayed (Acts 4:31; 12:12; 16:16; Eph. 6: 19-20; Phil. 1:19). Again and again their prayers were answered and spiritual victories were won. Indeed, prayer was a normal ingredient of life. Peter was praying when the messengers from Cornelius arrived (Acts 10:9) and the Antioch church—or, at least, its leadership—was praying when the Spirit's call to Barnabas and Saul was received. And as they sent the apostles forth they prayed again (Acts 13:1-3).

Prayers like those, prayers that count with God and contribute to effective mission, assume dependence on God. True prayer always depends on the praying subject surrendering himself, his work and his future to the will of God. He doesn't bargain with God. He doesn't ask God to bless choices he himself has made. Rather, he comes as a subject to his Sovereign and he comes in readiness to submit totally to his Sovereign's will. In prayer for mission, as in all true prayer, we dare not argue. We must submit to whatever answer the Lord may choose to give us.

Missionaries need power. And that power is in the person of the Spirit. They need his fullness, his control. Says the Lord Jesus, 'If you then . . . know how to give good gifts to your children, how much more will your Father in heaven give the Holy Spirit to those who ask him!' (Luke 11:13). The Christian needs to ask his heavenly Father not to receive the Holy Spirit—that has happened already—but that the Holy Spirit take full control of his life and empower him for witness. Ask then, pray then, that he will fill your life and infuse his power into your witness. The promise is clear: 'your Father in heaven will give the Holy Spirit to those who ask him'. We must pray, we must ask.

13
Guidance in mission

Missionary service is an exacting business. It produces situations that test and strain the missionary's sense of vocation. He can be tempted to pack his bags and take the next plane home!

At such times there is but one thing that can keep him at his task; an assurance that the situation in which he finds himself, trying as it may be, has come to him as he has followed God's call. He is where the Lord has sent him, and there can be no turning back.

How important then that, from the very beginning, the call be checked and that there be a firm assurance that the candidate is going forward in obedience to a real call from God. How tragic that of some it can be said, 'they went but were not sent'.

How does God guide?

God guides by various means:

1. Through common sense
God has given us powers of reasoning that enable us to weigh things up for ourselves. We can grasp principles and work out in our minds how they should affect our behaviour. We can to a degree look into the future and discern the consequences of doing this or that.

There are, of course, factors that work against us. We are limited in intelligence and we are not omniscient as is God. Our minds are also damaged and warped as a result of sin. We lack, therefore, the wisdom we need at times when important decisions have to be made. But the Christian can seek help from above. James says,'If any of you lacks wisdom, he should ask God, who gives generously to all without finding fault, and it will be given to him' (James 1:5).

Some very sincere Christians may see the idea of giving 'common sense' a role in guidance in our personal lives or in relation to mission like putting the cart before the horse! They would rather think in terms of some direct inner awareness that God was directing them in a particular direction. Yet dependence on common sense has warrant in Scripture. The apostle Paul in Antioch, after the first missionary journey and after the Jerusalem Council, became strongly desirous of revisiting the centres in Asia Minor in which converts had been won on his earlier journey. At the same time he had a row with Barnabas over John Mark (Acts 15:36ff.). He then chose Silas as his new companion and set off on the second missionary journey. There is no record of any supernatural guidance, and no suggestion that he was doing anything wrong, by acting without such guidance. Rather, it seems that in reasoning out what to do next he used his own wisdom, and in doing so was truly guided by God.

The same should surely be true of us today. We should use the reasoning powers that God has given us to survey our situations and to weigh up the possibilities and implications of a call—or possible call—to service. Issues like personal health and family commitments will be given careful consideration. Our circumstances will be accepted as of the Lord's ordering and as an important factor in the process of making a decision.

We cannot, of course, limit God. He may on occasions ask us to do exceptional things, things that do not at first seem wise or even possible. But, as a general rule, he works through the reasoning capacities he has given us and he expects us to act accordingly—in accordance with good, down-to-earth 'common sense'.

2. Through spiritual channels

The Holy Spirit resides in the believer. His role is to teach, to counsel, to lead into all truth. Those who have the Spirit can therefore be assured that he will contribute to their recognition of God's guidance. 'You . . . are controlled [guided] not by the sinful nature but by the Spirit, if the Spirit of God lives in you' (Rom. 8:9).

Prominent among the ways in which the Spirit guides are:

a) *Application of the Scriptures*

The author of Scripture himself interprets and applies it to men and women. He takes a word, a phrase, a sentence or a paragraph and uses it to arouse the conscience, to guide the soul. We can expect this to happen as we read the Bible or listen to it being read or expounded. In his high priestly prayer our Lord asked that his Father sanctify his disciples by the truth, 'your word', he said, 'is truth' (John 17:17). The word translated 'sanctify'means 'to set apart' and in the context of verses 15-23 refers to the setting apart of the disciples for witness in the world of men. What our Lord seems to affirm is that in calling his missionary servants God uses his Word. One would expect, therefore, that any call to missionary service would involve at some point a clear command from the Lord coming to the individual through the Scriptures.

This being so, our first priority is that we give the written word its proper place in our lives by studying and listening to it regularly. There is no substitute for a disciplined programme of day-by-day Bible study. It is hardly fair to expect real guidance through drawing promises from a special promise box or from opening a Bible at random and using a pointer to find a verse!

b) *The bestowal of gifts*

When God calls us to serve him he equips us with gifts appropriate to the task. It is a fundamental biblical principle that each believer receives some gift—'just as [the Spirit] determines' (1 Cor. 12:11). These gifts are for the common good (1 Cor. 12:7), for the edifying (the building up) of the body of Christ. They dictate the function of each believer within the body. For the missionary there may be a preaching or a teaching gift, one that equips for administration or for some specialist ministry. The prospective missionary must check that he has been given gift(s) appropriate to the tasks to which he proposes to lay his hand. To do this he will seek the help of mature and discerning fellow Christians, and especially of the elders in the church to which he belongs and in which he will already have served the Lord.

c) *The confirmation of other Christians*

A candidate is often quite unable to discern what his gifts are. To do so he needs the guidance and help of other Christians. Indeed, wherever in the New Testament we find men called to full-time service, we find that their call was confirmed and authenticated by Christians who knew them and who had the opportunity to see their gifts in operation. Saul and Barnabas had already ministered for a full year and were still doing so in Antioch (Acts 13:1-2). Timothy was valued and commended by the brothers at Lystra and Iconium who had observed his life and knew his gifts (Acts 16:2). The picture which emerges is of men who were active in their home churches and whose gifts were recognised there. When God's call to a wider ministry came, those home churches were in a position to confirm the guidance and to commit themselves to the support of the missionary.

Too many people today ignore or neglect their own churches. They render no service there and then, quite incongruously, expect those churches to support them as missionaries. Every prospective missionary should, as part of his preparation, have been deeply involved in the life of his home church and should—assuming it is a church which has spiritual life—be willing to accept its opinions and its dicipline in relation to his call.

Whom does God guide?

Scripture tells us that guidance can only come to those who fulfil specific conditions. Guidance is promised to:

1. Those who trust God

'Trust in the LORD with all your heart and lean not on your own understanding; in all your ways acknowledge him, and he will make your paths straight' (Prov. 3: 5-6).

To rely on one's own understanding is to exclude oneself from God's guidance. The Lord promises to instruct and teach and counsel the man who trusts in him. He leads such along right paths.

You want guidance? Tell the Lord that you trust him to guide you, to lead you along the right path, and mean it as did the Psalmist,who said, 'as for me, I trust in you' (Ps. 55:23).

2. Those who are humble
'He guides the humble in what is right and teaches them his way' (Ps. 25:9).

Humility is an attitude of submission before God. It is the opposite of arrogance and pride. It involves teachability and a readiness to be corrected. It is brokenness and poverty of spirit before the Lord.

You want guidance? 'Submit yourselves, then, to God . . . Humble yourselves before the Lord' (Jas. 4:7,10).

3. Those who obey God
I will instruct you and teach you in the way you should go;
   I will counsel you and watch over you.
Do not be like the horse or the mule
   which have no understanding
but must be controlled by bit and bridle
   or they will not come to you (Ps. 32:8-9)

Those who are not willingly obedient, who need to be controlled by physical restraints, don't get instruction or guidance in the way they should go. It is almost as if God has to overrule their circumstances and force them to do what he wants!

Willing, glad and spontaneous obedience is what God wants from every one of his children. It is those who choose to do his will who are given more light, and who thus find confirmation that teaching or guidance is coming from him (cf. John 17:17). Obedience is crucial.

You want guidance? Throughout your life, obey God. As Mary the mother of Jesus said, 'Do whatever he tells you' (John 2:5).

Guidance is never easy. While it begins with common sense, the spiritual dimension must be given its proper place. The Holy Spirit must enlighten our minds and be allowed to speak to us both by working in us and through the discernment of our fellow believers. We must meet the conditions: trust the Lord; humble yourself; obey God.

14
The missionary's resources

The early missionaries did not have things easy. They took on
the self-righteousness of the Jewish world and the licen-
tiousness of the Graeco-Roman world and often paid the price as
they suffered indignities and even martyrdom. What kept them
going?

The Lord on whom they depended

The apostolic missionaries depended totally on God. This is
shown by:

1. His power in their work

The Lord demonstrated his power through the missionaries. A
lame man was healed (3:1-11) and so were Aeneas, a paralytic (9:32-
35), and the father of Publius who suffered from a feverish illness
(28:8). Dorcas was even raised from the dead (9:36-41). Peter and
John, Peter again, and Paul and Silas were miraculously released
from prison. At the same time men and women were converted
from a stubborn Judaism (e.g. Paul, Lydia, and others) and from
a licentious paganism (1 Cor. 6:9-11).

In his speech at Pentecost Peter had quoted Joel's prophecy of
'wonders' in the heavens and 'signs' on the earth. In the same context he proclaimed that Jesus had been accredited by miracles,
'wonders and signs' (Greek, *terata kai semeia*, Acts 2:19 and 22).
In fact this phrase occurs nine times in Acts (see also 2:43; 4:30;
5:12; 7:36; 8:13; 14:3; 15:12).

The miracles were, indeed, extraordinary (19:11). They were
'power-encounters' through which men come into contact with
God. They were also evidence that God approved of and was
working through the messengers. They were signs of his presence

and power and at the same time marks of a true apostle. Thus Paul referring to his own ministry in Corinth could say,

I am not in the least inferior to the 'super-apostles', even though I am nothing. The things that mark an apostle—signs, wonders and miracles—were done among you [i.e. by himself] with great perseverance (2 Cor. 12:11f.).

Putting this evidence together it is clear that the mission of the early church was carried out under the sovereign control of the Holy Spirit.

2. The overrulings of providence

Divinely ordained providences provided the missionaries with contacts and opportunities: they found themselves in the right places at the right times. Thus Peter and John met a cripple at the temple gate (3:1). The opening of prison gates (5:19; 12:10; 16:26) thus became opportunities. So too were the threats of violence and persecution that contributed to the spread of the gospel (8:4; 9:23; 13:50f.; 14:19; 17:10,14; 20:1). The missionaries knew that in all things God was working for the good of those who love him (Rom. 8:28) and so accepted whatever providences came their way. Paul could say of his imprisonment in Rome, 'what has happened to me has really served to advance the gospel' (Phil. 1:12-14).

3. The metaphors they used of themselves

The terms the apostles used to describe themselves and their work show that they were not in business for their own benefit but as servants dependent on the Lord. They were ministers through whom converts like those in Corinth had been led to faith. They might sow the seed of divine truth and even water it, but they could not make it germinate—they depended on God to make it grow (1 Cor. 3:5-9).

Designations like steward (1 Cor. 4:1 AV), ambassador (2 Cor. 5:20), and soldier (1 Cor. 9:7) similarly stress the fact that the missionary is dependent on and responsible to the Lord who sends him out as his representative.

4. Their ascriptions of glory to God

Because they were dependent servants of God the apostolic missionaries never took glory for the success of their work. They constantly insisted that all the honour, the good reputation, the glory (Greek, *doxa*), be ascribed to God, 'To him be the glory for ever!' (Rom. 11:36; cf. Gal. 1:5; 2 Tim. 4:18; Heb. 13:21; Jude 25).

Paul expressed this concern in highly personal terms: 'I glory in Christ Jesus in my service to God. I will not venture to speak of anything except what Christ has accomplished through me . . .' (Rom. 15:17f.). He could tell the Thessalonians that he and his colleagues 'were not looking for praise (Greek, *doxa*) from men, not from you or anyone else' (1 Thess. 2:6). Ascribing all honour for what was accomplished through their work to God, they showed that they were his servants working for his benefit and depending entirely on him.

5. Their constant resort to prayer

In the Acts alone we learn that prayer played an important part in mission. Not many prayers are recorded, but we find the apostles and their associates praying in a wide variety of situations. They seem to have turned almost automatically to communion with their Lord. They prayed:

a) *When the Spirit's presence and power were needed or awaited*
When, for example, a successor to Judas was being chosen and when Peter and John arrived in Samaria (1:14; 8:14f.), they prayed.

b) *When spiritual victories had been won*
The conversions at Pentecost and the release of Peter and John from the Sanhedrin resulted in prayer to God (2:42; 4:24-30).

c) *When new workers were chosen or commissioned*
Matthias, the seven, and Saul and Barnabas are examples (1:24f.; 6:6; 13:3).

d) *When workers left a sphere of service*
Their departure meant that converts had to continue the work of evangelism and church building. Prayer was then appropriate (14:23; 20:36;21:5).

e) *When there was crisis or challenge*

When Stephen faced death, when Ananias was instructed to visit Saul in Damascus, when Dorcas had died, when Peter was imprisoned in Jerusalem, and when Paul and Silas were spending a night in prison in Philippi, prayer was spontaneously offered (7:59f.; 9:10-14; 9:40; 12:5,12; 16:25).

f) *When things were normal*

Thus Peter prayed on the roof-top in Joppa and Paul and his colleagues went 'to the place of prayer' at Philippi with the obvious intention that there they would engage in prayer (10:9; 16:16).

Then we have a number of significant prayers and requests for prayer recorded in the epistles. Paul, for example, prays for the strengthening of his Ephesian readers (Eph. 3:16-19) and asks them in turn to pray for him that even though he is in chains he may be fearless in making the gospel known (Eph. 6:19f.). He assured the Philippians and the Colossians of his prayers for them (Phil. 1:3-6,9-11; Col. 1:9-13). A similar pattern is found in his letters to the Thessalonians—he assures them of his prayers (1 Thess. 1:2f.; 2 Thess. 1:11f.) and he asks them to pray for him (1 Thess. 5:25). Writing to Timothy in relation to the life of the church in Ephesus he urges that prayers be made for everyone, and especially for those in authority, so that God's purpose of saving souls might be facilitated (1 Tim. 2:1-4).

These prayers showed the dependence of the missionaries on God. They knew to whom they should and could turn in every situation of need. After Pentecost their prayers were a factor in bringing a feeling of awe to Jerusalem and in the conversion of souls (Acts 2:42-47). After Peter and John were released from prison the disciples prayed with wonderful confidence in God (Acts 4:24-30) and following that were filled with the Spirit and equipped to speak God's word boldly (4:31). Their prayer life was integral to their effectiveness in mission.

The prayers of the apostles were also closely related to the receipt of divine guidance. The vision that made Peter's mind open to going to Cornelius was guidance received in the context of prayer (10:9ff.). Much later Paul told how on an early visit to Jerusalem he had been praying and had fallen into a trance in which he received guidance to leave the city. That had been a turning point in his career—he learned that he was being sent to the Gentiles (22:17-21).

The New Testament shows, then, that dependence on God was the early missionaries' supreme resource. Mission is God's work, and if a missionary fails to give God full sovereignty over it and fails to depend on him for his message, for his guidance, for his support, for everything, he ceases to be a missionary in the sense in which the New Testament understands the term.

The churches supporting them

The missionaries were called by God and sent out by their home churches (Acts 13:1-4; 16:1-5; cf. 1 Tim. 1:18; 4:14). The sending church at Antioch maintained an interest in Paul and his colleagues and on two occasions the apostle returned there and spent time and shared news of his work with it. Of the first and longer visit we read:

> they sailed back to Antioch, where they had been committed to the grace of God for the work they had now completed. On arriving there, they gathered the church together and reported all that God had done through them . . . (Acts 14:26ff.; cf. 18:22f.)

Paul was, at least on this first occasion, received back into the ministry team of the church and took the leading role in the ensuing discussions with Jerusalem over the status of Gentile believers (14:26–15:35). However, as time went on his links with Antioch seem to have weakened and, as we read his letters, we see him in fellowship with and supported by a whole group of churches. He depended on and, indeed, asked for their prayers— 'Pray also for me . . .' (Eph. 6:19). The churches did pray for him (2 Cor. 1:11) and in the case of Philippi sent money to him on more

131

than one occasion (Phil. 4:16). The apostle certainly had good support from the various churches amongst which he moved.

In addition, the strong bonds of fellowship among the missionaries and between them and church members, as evidenced by the greetings in many of the epistles, indicate a great deal of mutual support. Christian fellowship was an important missionary resource.

Their own dedication

Dedication to the task of evangelism or mission characterised the early missionaries. Stephen and James were both faithful to the point of death (7:57–8:1; 12:2). Even Mark, who was an initial disappointment (Acts 13:13; 15:36-39), did not totally give up, but continued in mission with Barnabas with whom he went to Cyprus (v. 39). Later he was rehabilitated into Paul's circle and proved himself useful to the apostle (2 Tim. 4:11). His heart must have been dedicated to the Lord and if, as is generally believed, he is the author of our second Gospel, there can be no doubt about that dedication—his concern in writing it was to record and proclaim 'the gospel about Jesus Christ, the Son of God' (Mark 1:1).

Paul himself suffered much for the sake of the gospel. He had been under such great pressure that he had despaired even of life itself (2 Cor. 1:8). He was imprisoned, flogged, stoned, shipwrecked, hungry, thirsty, cold and exposed to death again and again. He had been in danger in cities, in the countryside and at sea, and even from false brothers (2 Cor. 11:23-29). Yet he persevered and, as far as we know, like Stephen and James, was martyred. He never lost his enthusiasm for the gospel and could write, '. . . I am compelled to preach. Woe to me if I do not preach the gospel!' (1 Cor. 9:16). His dedication was such that he and his colleagues shared not only the gospel but their own lives with those to whom they ministered (1 Thess. 2:8). Paul was, indeed, a man of single-minded dedication to the commission he had received from the Lord—'one thing I do' (Phil. 3:13f.). At the end of his life he could face death knowing he had fulfilled God's will—'I have fought the good fight, I have finished the race, I have kept the faith . . .' (2 Tim. 4:7f.). What a testimony! What dedication of heart!

A dedicated heart is a vital resource without which no one will persevere in mission. It is men and women with dedication like that of the early missionaries whom God uses in mission.

Consistency of life and message

In mission, as in every form of ministry for the Lord, lifestyle plays an important role. The missionary's job is to urge people to turn to the Lord and to a life of righteousness. If he does not display that righteousness in his own life, his message, his work and the Lord are denied. As has been said, 'The quality of a missionary's life either enriches or emasculates the message.' His way of life can, then, mightily reinforce or mercilessly negate the message. It must involve both true godliness and true righteousness.

1. Godliness

English dictionaries define godliness in terms of being devout, religious or pious. From a biblical perspective godliness certainly involves these characteristics, but somehow they are seriously inadequate. True godliness is not just a matter of going through the motions of religious devotion. It is a matter of the heart, of knowing God and of being known by God (John 17:3; Gal. 4:9, etc.).

Godliness is first and foremost a relationship between the soul and the Lord. In that relationship the soul communes with God through prayer and by receiving and meditating on his Word. So far as missionaries are concerned, a vital and an ongoing communion with the Lord is an absolute prerequisite of effective service. They must be men and women of prayer, men and women who feed on God's Word, who are themselves examples of the godliness they expect converts to espouse and display.

2. Righteousness

Nothing is more effective in backing up the gospel than the

display of truly Christian—Christlike—behaviour. The Lord's servants entrusted with the gospel are responsible to live it out in consistently righteous lives.

It was the Lord Jesus himself, who said, 'let your light shine before men, that they may see your good deeds and praise your Father in heaven' (Matt. 5:16). He was saying that good deeds, actions that are truly righteous and have the added quality of goodness, bear their own testimony and contribute greatly towards turning hearts towards the Lord.

As a missionary Timothy was to 'set an example for the believers in speech, in life, in love, in faith and in purity' (1 Tim. 4:12). Righteous living was vital to his mission, and to maintain this he must flee from evils like those arising from a love of money, and must positively 'pursue righteousness, godliness, faith, love, endurance and gentleness' (1 Tim. 6:11). Writing to Titus, then on a missionary assignment in Crete, Paul similarly urged him to set an example by doing what is good. 'In your teaching', he added, 'show integrity, seriousness and soundness of speech that cannot be condemned,.so that those who oppose you may be ashamed because they have nothing bad to say about us' (Tit. 2:7-8).

Peter argued along the same lines, telling his readers that they had been chosen to declare the praises of the one who had called them. He urged them to abstain from sinful desires and to live good lives among the pagans so that, even if they were accused of doing wrong, their accusers would see their good works and in the end glorify God (1 Pet. 2:9-12). Later he pleaded that they keep their consciences clear (i.e. by avoiding unrighteous behaviour) so that those who spoke maliciously against them might be ashamed of the slanderous statements they had made (1 Pet. 3:16).

If good conduct truly in accord with the biblical ethic is a vital constituent of missionary work, the corollary is that bad behaviour, especially when attributable to evangelising or missioning Christians, is extremely damaging to the cause of Christ. Even in Old Testament times God was deeply concerned about priests and prophets whose task was the spreading of his word but who followed an evil and a godless course—'from the prophets of Jerusalem ungodliness has spread throughout the land' (Jer. 23:15).

In the Acts we learn of one man, Simon, who had been a popular sorcerer in Samaria and who, after professing to believe in Christ, offered money to the apostles to purchase spiritual power. Peter responded by telling him that he could have no part or share in the ministry of missionary evangelism because his heart was not right before God. Before he could share in such ministry he must repent and seek God's forgiveness (Acts 8:18-24). Thus attitudes and activities out of harmony with the message disqualify a person from missionary work and call for his or her repentance before God. In a word, the messenger must be right with God.

Paul's choice of Timothy as a junior member of his team (Acts 16:2) was of a young man of whom the leaders of the churches in Lystra and Iconium 'spoke well'. Obviously his lifestyle was harmonious with the message and with the mission of the apostle. The important thing thereafter was that he keep it so—'I charge you to keep this command without spot or blame until the appearing of our Lord Jesus Christ' (1Tim. 6:13f.).

Clearly, then, the New Testament picture of missionaries is of people who practised what they preached, whose devotional life was healthy and whose general conduct was truly ethical. They were both godly and righteous and, being so, their lifestyle magnified and gave authority to the good news they proclaimed.

15
Why mission?

We must now attempt to assemble the New Testament evidence about why the 'missionary endeavour' we have examined was carried on.

We want to discover what motivated the early missionaries and in doing so to discover reasons why we should follow in the steps of those who pioneered mission.

Obedience

This is basic to mission, as it is to all aspects of Christian life.

1. Obedience to the commands of Christ

Our examination of the 'Goals of Mission' in chapter 8 paid considerable attention to the Great Commission and to the responsibility it imposes on Christians to proclaim the good news, to plant churches and to instruct disciples.

> . . . go and make disciples of all nations, baptising them in the name of the Father and of the Son and of the Holy Spirit, and teaching them to obey everything I have commanded you (Matt. 28:19f.).

While we don't need to repeat what was said earlier we must keep the commission of Jesus at the heart of our missionary motivation.

Christians are always under obligation to obey the commands of Jesus—as Paul put it, we are 'under Christ's law' (1 Cor. 9:21). Because this is so we cannot evade and must not neglect missionary endeavour. Obedience to what the Lord Jesus commanded is our basic duty and the basis of a proper ongoing relationship with him—'If you obey my commands, you will remain in my love . . .' (John 15:10). In the nature of things, then, obedience to Christ's Great Commission must be a basic element in the motivation to mission.

2. Obedience to the exhortations of the apostles

There is no equivalent to our Lord's great commission in the Epistles or the Revelation, but there are several emphases which are mission-related and which become virtual exhortations to missionary evangelism.

a) *About preaching*

The message of the cross—the word preached or proclaimed—is God's method of saving those who believe (1 Cor. 1:18,21). In Romans 10 Paul emphasises that people must hear before they can believe and in order to hear they need a preacher, one who is sent to proclaim the good news, whether to groups or to individuals. In what was probably his very last letter Paul told Timothy that he should 'not be ashamed to testify about our Lord' and that he should 'do the work of an evangelist' (2 Tim. 1:8; 4:5). The purpose of proclamation is to make Christ known—is, in fact, mission.

b) *About praying*

The apostles' prayers and their requests for prayer (examined earlier) mostly relate in some way to the spread of the gospel and so have missionary significance both in their intention and in their effect. When the apostles prayed and their prayers were answered, there was more boldness in speech, more liberty to preach and more stamina to endure hardship. The fact that prayer had a prominent place in the lives of the apostles, and in particular in relation to their mission, highlights the importance and the imperative of mission.

c) *About behaving*

The New Testament is full of teaching on Christian behaviour.

What is important in the context of mission is the way in which the behaviour of a Christian either enhances or emasculates witness. Because this is the case Paul told the Colossians to be wise in the way they acted towards outsiders and to be gracious in conversation so as to make the most of every opportunity (Col. 4:5f.). He reminded the Corinthians that their lives are like a letter that all can read (2 Cor. 3:2f.). Peter also spoke about the effect of behaviour on witness—good behaviour can silence accusers and can lead some to give glory to God (1 Pet. 2:12-15; 3:16). The lesson is that because our lives bear a testimony in favour of or against the Lord, we must by consistent Christian behaviour make our witness positive rather than negative.

Emulation

In the New Testament we are called to emulate our Lord and his apostles.

1. The example of Jesus

In an earlier study Jesus was presented as Missionary Supreme. He above all others was 'sent' by God, was God's missionary, 'the apostle . . . whom we confess' (Heb. 3:1). The way in which he sought to reach men and women provided a compelling pattern for the apostles who first received his commission, and for whom his own practice of mission was wonderful training for it. Their task was to emulate—to follow the example of—him who said, 'As the Father has sent me, I am sending you' (John 20:21).

While many of those who were helped and blessed through our Lord's ministry deliberately sought him out, the basic fact was that he, the Son of Man, came to seek and to save those who were lost (Luke 19:10). Though Zacchaeus was curious to see him and had put himself as near as possible to him, it was, in fact, Jesus who was seeking him—'I must stay at your house today' (Luke 19:5).

By taking the culturally unpopular route from Jerusalem to Galilee via Samaria, the Lord made contact with an immoral woman who came to faith in him as Messiah and who herself became a witness to the citizens of Samaria (John 4). Back in Jerusalem he approached and then healed the man who had been an invalid for 38 years (John 5:6).

Our Lord's threefold parable of lostness—the lost sheep, the lost coin and the lost sons (Luke 15) illustrates his own and, indeed, his Father's way of seeking men and women who are not in a living relationship with God. And as he was sent to seek the lost, so in every subsequent age he sends his disciples to seek the lost. His example ought to motivate and be emulated by his disciples in every generation.

2. The example of the apostles

As we read the New Testament we cannot fail to be impressed by the eager zeal of the early missionaries. They sought to follow the example set by the Lord, and they in turn become part of the pattern for mission provided in Scripture for succeeding generations.

Peter and those with him at Pentecost and in the months and years that followed set the stage. Next we find Stephen who preached fearlessly even when faced with martyrdom. Then we learn how those scattered by persecution 'preached the word wherever they went' and how Philip did so in Samaria and at Gaza. These first missionaries show us how those who have grasped the significance of the gospel can and should become enthusiastic missionaries.

The chronicle of Paul's ministry as recorded by Luke in Acts 13–28 shows his absolute commitment to and zeal for the task of mission. He was one who, to use Peter's words, was always 'prepared to give an answer to everyone who asks . . . the reason for the hope that you have' (1 Pet. 3:15). He did just that at Antioch in Pisidia, with the jailer in Philippi and with the philosophers in Athens (Acts 13:15ff.; 16:29ff.; 17:19ff.). He was also ready to speak about the Lord even when no one asked him to do so, as was the case in some synagogues and with Lydia (Acts 16:13ff.).

The apostolic missionaries pressed the claims of Christ on Greek and non-Greek, on the wise and the foolish, and regarded the gospel as God's power for salvation for all alike. The message was that 'Everyone who calls on the name of the Lord will be saved' (Rom. 1:14-16; 10:11-13; cf. Acts 13:46; 17:1-15). The apostles looked for those like Lydia at Philippi whose hearts were being opened by the Lord, but never once do we find them missing an opportunity to proclaim the message to those they met, whatever their race, creed or social status.

The apostles had missionary hearts. They preached the good news of Christ and in doing so gave themselves to the spiritual and eternal welfare of those who came under their influence. Their example is part of God's revelation of his will to us and, therefore, of the imperative that rests on us and that ought always to be a motive for mission.

Responsibility

Our responsibility is awesome:

1. For the unsaved facing perdition

Our Lord presented a very solemn picture of the destiny awaiting those who died without God's forgiveness and salvation. As early as the Sermon on the Mount he pointed out that there would be those who used his name and who addressed him as Lord who would ultimately be excluded from the kingdom of heaven. He will then tell such, 'I never knew you. Away from me, you evildoers' (Matt. 7:21-23). Because of this he was concerned that his hearers (then and now) would enter the gate that is small and walk the narrow road that leads to life (Matt. 7:13f.).

Later in Jesus' ministry he made the doom of the unrighteous even clearer. He insisted that there would be a solemn judgment for all mankind. At this the unrighteous will be separated from the righteous (as goats are separated from sheep) and will be consigned to the eternal fire prepared for the devil and his angels—'they will go away to eternal punishment' (Matt. 24:31; 25:31-46). He even described this as being 'thrown into hell, where "their worm does not die and the fire is not quenched"' (Mark 9:47f.). For him the majority of men and women travel a road 'that leads to destruction' (Matt. 7:13). He had a deep burden, a real concern for such—he had been sent into the world that the people of the world might be saved through him (John 3:17). He had come to seek and to save the lost (Luke 19:10).

His concern to save people meant that he had to give up his life for them—'Greater love has no-one than this, that he lay down his life for his friends' (John 15:13). His love—his loving concern—sets an example that many Christians have followed over the centuries and that all Christians should be willing to emulate.

The apostles were equally sure that an awful fate awaited the ungodly and were deeply concerned to see them saved from it. Thus Paul speaks of the ungodly as 'those who are perishing': that is, as being on a road that leads to eternal perdition or doom (1 Cor. 1:18; 2 Cor. 2:15; 4:3). He uses the present participle in order to show that those to whom he refers are moving in the direction of perdition—they will inevitably perish unless they repent or change direction. Elsewhere he speaks of those who are 'without hope and without God in the world' (Eph. 2:12), people who are under God's wrath (Eph. 2:3; 5:6) and liable to suffer exclusion 'from the presence of the Lord . . . [when] he comes to be glorified in his holy people' (2 Thess. 1:9).

Peter says that God holds the unrighteous for the day of judgment, a day of destruction for ungodly men, a day of perdition (2 Pet. 2:9; 3:7-9). The writer to the Hebrews insists that all must face judgment and speaks of God as 'a consuming fire' (Heb. 9:27; 12:29). The outpouring of God's wrath on the ungodly is also vividly portrayed in the Revelation—'tormented with burning sulphur' (14:9-11).

The New Testament writers thus unite to show that an awful doom faces the unsaved. They also show clearly that God's concern is to prevent men from meeting such a terrible destiny by saving them through Christ. He does not want 'anyone to perish, but everyone to come to repentance' (2 Pet. 3:9). It is, then, as an expression of concern that he calls the church in general and missionaries in particular. Their task and their duty are to share his burden and take upon themselves the responsibility of

142

seeking out and persuading those who are perishing.

Paul told the elders of Ephesus that he had served the Lord among them 'with tears' and that, as he bade them a final farewell, he was confident that he was 'innocent of the blood of all men' (Acts 20:19,26). It would seem that he was casting himself in a role similar to that of Ezekiel, namely that of a watchman whose responsibility was to warn people of impending danger and who would be guilty of their blood if he failed to do so. Paul had shown such concern for the salvation of his friends that he was sure he bore no such guilt. How many Christians today would dare make such a confident assertion?

Paul's deep concern for the salvation of others is shown in a different way in his first letter to the Corinthians. He tells them that he had become 'all things to all men so that by all possible means [he] might save some' (1 Cor. 9:22). He had left no stone unturned in his efforts to persuade men to repent and be saved. He was deeply burdened and wanted to be nothing other than an instrument through which others would find deliverance from the doom awaiting all unbelievers.

The words of James strike a similar note—'Whoever turns a sinner from the error of his way will save him from death . . .' (Jas. 5:20). The terrible destiny awaiting the unsaved makes the proclamation of the gospel imperative. Knowing that it is a dreadful thing to fall into the hands of the living God, we, like Paul, ought to feel burdened for the eternal welfare of our fellow human beings and ought to be compelled, as he was, to persuade them (2 Cor. 5:10f.).

2. For the glory or honour of God

Discussing the 'Goals of Mission' we observed that bringing glory to God must be the supreme reason for being involved in mission. That being so, the desire to see God's honour increased as people come to faith must be the major element in the motivation of mission.

When Paul and Barnabas turned to them, the Gentiles in Pisidian Antioch 'honoured [or glorified] the word of the Lord'

(Acts 13:48). Later Paul asked the Thessalonian Christians to pray that the message might spread rapidly and be honoured just as it had been with the Thessalonians themselves (2 Thess. 3:1). The honouring of God's Word was clearly an honouring of the Lord from whom it came. Similarly Paul prayed that the name of the Lord Jesus might be glorified in his Thessalonian friends (2 Thess. 1:12).

Peter, urging his readers to use the gifts God had given them, said that anyone who spoke should do it as 'speaking the very words of God . . . so that in all things God may be praised [glorified AV, RSV; Greek, *doxazo*]' (1 Pet. 4:11). Jude's doxology strikes the same note and focuses the emphasis of the entire New Testament that in all things God might be glorified—'to the only God our Saviour be glory . . . now and for evermore!' (Jude v. 25). That God will be glorified must always be the burden of those called to mission.

Thankfulness

The idea of thankfully responding to God's love and grace by rendering him service is found throughout the New Testament. Our Lord, commenting on the case of a sinful woman who had anointed his feet with expensive ointment, pointed out that one who had been forgiven a great debt would love the one forgiving him more than someone released from a small debt (Luke 7:41-42). It is likely that such gratitude motivated the witness of the Samaritan woman to whom Jesus revealed his Messiahship—she left her water pot and went into Samaria saying, 'Come, see . . .' (John 4:26-29).

In general terms Paul urged his readers to present themselves to God as living sacrifices, that is, as available to him for service (Rom. 12:1). And the reason for this is 'God's mercy'. Paul is saying that what his readers had experienced of the mercies of God, which he had surveyed and expounded earlier in the letter, demanded that in thankfulness they make themselves available for worship/service.

Paul saw himself as the least of the apostles—the least of the early missionaries—one who did not deserve to be an apostle but who was one by virtue of the grace of God (1 Cor. 15:9-11). In a further letter to the Corinthians he said that Christ's love, the love that caused 'one to die for all,' compelled him and his colleagues. It left them no choice other than to proclaim the message of reconciliation and to implore men to be reconciled to God (2 Cor. 5:11-21). Later still, he specifically thanked the Lord for the fact that, despite his background, he had been called to service and given strength for the tasks he faced as an apostle and missionary (1 Tim. 1:12ff.). Thankfulness was obviously prominent in his thinking and in his motivation.

Another apostle majors on the fact that God is love and, as such, requires that his servants love one another. For John, love for fellow believers and for those who are not yet believers is generated in response to God's love: 'We love because he first loved us' (1 John 4:19). In the same passage John also says, 'we have seen and testify that the Father has sent his Son to be the Saviour of the world' (1 John 4:14). Clearly what God has done for sinful men and women serves to motivate those who experience his love to bear witness to his salvation. In a word, thankfulness motivates mission.

What then are the motives for mission? Obedience, emulation of Christ and the apostles, concern for the unsaved and for the glory of God and genuine thankfulness motivate mission. 'The love of Christ leaves us no choice' (2 C or. 5:14a NEB).

Appendix A
Crossing barriers of culture and race

' "Nazareth! Can anything good come from there?" Nathanael asked' (John 1:46). By that snide question he revealed that there was a cultural barrier between himself and the inhabitants of Nazareth. Such barriers have existed since the earliest of times and are, of course, introduced to us by the Tower of Babel story (Gen. 11:7-9).

The Old Testament background

The Old Testament provides us with some helpful material.

1. The curse on Ham
Many white people, especially in Southern Africa, believe that the curse pronounced in Genesis 9:18-27 was imposed not just on Canaan, the son of Ham, but on the entire black race. Some also believe it to mean that black people are destined to be inferior to whites.

The theory is thoroughly illogical. It makes Egypt (the land of Ham—Pss. 105:27; 106:22) the link between the curse and the negroid people of sub-Saharan Africa. But, in fact, the curse was pronounced on one son of Ham (therefore the grandson or youngest son of Noah), Canaan. And the descendants of Canaan were the Canaanites, in whose land the Israelites later settled, and had no connection at all with Africa. They were also white and belonged to what anthropologists know as the Caucasoid, Great White or Indo-European Race, as were the Egyptians and all the people of Northern Africa! Whatever the outworking of Noah's curse (if it had any outworking!) it was not black skin and it was not Negroid blood. Scripture does not claim that the curse pronounced by Noah in the aftermath of drunken stupor was a divine pronouncement or that it was one that had to be, or was, implemented by God. Even if it is regarded as part of the divine intention it can be argued with considerable cogency that it found its fulfilment in the destruction of the various Canaanite tribes as a result of divine command when Israel entered the land.

2. Israelite treatment of non-Israelites

The Mosaic law insisted that strangers were not to be oppressed. Rather they were to be loved and treated with real kindness. They were to have the benefits of Sabbath rest and of gleanings from the crops (Exod. 22:21; 23:9; Lev. 19:9-10; 23:22). They could even use the cities of refuge (Num. 35:15; Deut. 10:19; 24:19ff.; Josh. 20:9). If, however, a stranger wished to participate in the Passover, he was required to become an Israelite through circumcision (Exod. 12:48).

The other side of the coin is that the Israelites were required to maintain separation from the religion of pagan tribes; Baal worship and every form of idolatry were forbidden territory. Inter-racial marriages were a factor which often threatened the purity of religion (e.g. 1 Kgs 11:1-8). Because of their negative effect on religion and morality such marriages were actually dissolved under Ezra and Nehemiah at the end of the Old Testament era (Ezra 9; Neh. 13:23-28; cf. Mal. 2:13-16). This emphasis on religious purity undoubtedly contributed to the exclusivism and in some cases to a sense of racial superiority which developed over many centuries of Jewish life.

There were, however, other strands of thought at work. In chapter 2 we noticed some of the implications of the book of Jonah. The prophet resented the fact that God called him to missionary work in Nineveh, the capital city of his people's arch enemies, the Assyrians. He had to learn the hard way, as we would say, that God loved non-Israelites and wanted to spare them from perdition. His challenging question to Jonah was, 'Should I not be concerned about that great city?' (Jon. 4:11). He was

147

concerned about the Ninevites, and Jonah and all who read the book that bears his name should be equally concerned to reach out in love to people of races other that their own.

Jeremiah's life was saved by the compassionate action of an Ethiopian or Cushite named Ebed-Melech (Jer. 38:7-13). Cush or biblical Ethiopia was the southern part of Egypt, now known as Northern Sudan and not the modern Ethiopia. Ebed-Melech was probably therefore a descendant of Ham and of a different race from the Semitic Israelites. Yet he trusted in the Lord and was therefore promised divine protection when Jerusalem would fall to the Babylonians—'I will save you . . . because you trust in me, declares the LORD' (Jer. 39:15-18). Thus God's love and saving grace reached out across racial barriers and were not entirely confined to Israelites.

3. Predictions of Gentiles coming to faith

When God called Abraham he promised that he would bless the peoples of the earth through him and through his offspring (Gen. 12:3). Centuries later the prophets were able confidently to proclaim that foreigners would seek the God of Israel and would want to be instructed in his ways—the promised blessing would be theirs.

In the last days the mountain of the LORD's temple will be . . . raised above the hills, and all nations will stream to it. Many peoples will come and say, 'Come, let us go up to the mountain of the LORD, to the house of the God of Jacob. He will teach us his ways, so that we may walk in his paths' (Isa. 2:2-3; cf. Ezek. 47:21-23, etc.).

Such predictions point to a new order in which differences of culture would be transcended among people who have a common faith in God, the Lord.

The ministry of our Lord

The existence of sects within Judaism meant that there were cultural barriers dividing those to whom our Lord ministered. The

Sadducees were an upper-crust elite almost entirely made up of influential priestly families. The Pharisees were a cult of self-righteous pietists who despised as 'sinners' those Jews who did not or could not conform to their pernickety rules. The differences between them normally kept them apart.

The area of land lying between Judea and Galilee was populated by people whose ancestry involved a mix of Israelites with peoples introduced to the area by the Assyrians after their conquest of Samaria in 722 BC (2 Kgs. 17:24-40). They, the Samaritans, had the five books of Moses and, despite the introduction of pagan blood, established and maintained considerable reverence for God. For several centuries they even had their own temple on Mount Gerizim. This had been destroyed by John Hyrcanus late in the second century BC, an action which increased the animosity between them and the Jews and kept the two groups apart—'Jews do not associate with Samaritans' (John 4:9).

Racial animosity meant that a self-respecting Jew would not travel through Samaria but would add some fifty or sixty miles to his journey by taking the route along the east bank of the river Jordan. However, our Lord defied convention and the cultural barrier and travelled through Samaria—'he had to go through Samaria' (John 4:4). He did so because there he would win the allegiance of a Samaritan woman and as a result of her conversion see many Samaritans come to believe in him (John 4:39-42). He crossed the cultural and racial barrier that separated the two communities with a clear missionary objective in his mind.

On another occasion (Matt. 15:21-28) Jesus went to the region of Tyre and Sidon, where he encountered a Canaanite woman who addressed him as 'Lord' and as 'Son of David'. By doing so she was, it seems, using Jewish titles and in all probability pretending to be a Jewess in the hope that she would have a better chance of receiving help from him. His initial silence and his insistence that he was sent only to the lost sheep of Israel appear rather harsh but, in fact, seem to have been his way of forcing the woman to be honest and acknowledge that she was non-Israelite. When honesty was established he responded instantly to her plea and healed her daughter. Again a barrier of culture and of race had been crossed.

While our Lord's mission was, in fact, primarily directed towards Jews in Galilee and Judea, it was not restricted to them. Indeed he predicted that people from east and west, north and south would join with Abraham and the saints of old in the kingdom of God, while evildoers of Israelite nationality would be excluded (Luke 13:28-30). In the Great Commission he told his disciples to make disciples in all nations (Matt. 28:19 etc.). The gospel was not for any one culture or race but for 'all nations' and the barriers of culture and of race would be transcended by it.

The ministry of the apostles

On the Day of Pentecost God-fearing Jews from every corner of the Middle East heard in their own languages the preaching of the apostolic band (Acts 2:8-11). Clearly they shared a common Judaism, but there would also be cultural differences as great as, if not greater than, those dividing Galileans from Judeans and both of these from the Samaritans. In addition to local vernacular languages, many of the pilgrims to Jerusalem would have spoken Greek as their lingua franca rather than the Aramaic then in common use in Judea. The effect of the different languages and of the cultural baggage that accompanied them was soon evident when tension arose over the distribution of alms to widows—'the Grecian Jews among them complained against the Hebraic Jews because their widows were being overlooked in the daily distribution of food' (Acts 6:1).

New problems arose when Gentiles in considerable numbers became Christians at Antioch and in the churches of the first missionary journey (Acts 11:19-26; 13,14). Christian Jews with a Pharisaic bent went from Jerusalem to Antioch, and probably also to Galatia, telling Gentile converts that it was not enough to believe in Christ; they must also submit to circumcision and, therefore, to the whole corpus of Jewish Rabbinic law. The council of Jerusalem (Acts 15:1-31) discussed the problem and ruled against the Judaisers and advised the Gentile believers that they did not need to become Jews.

Writing to the Galatian churches Paul made the same point, insisting that all believers, whether of Jewish or non-Jewish background, are 'sons of God through faith in Christ Jesus'. He went on to assert that in Christ there is neither Jew nor Greek, because all are one in Christ Jesus, and that those who belong to Christ—even Gentile believers—are Abraham's (spiritual) offspring (Gal. 3:26-29). This being so, circumcision and the Jewish religion and the nationality it symbolised had no significance in terms of Christianity; the only things that count are faith expressing itself through love and a new creation (Gal. 5:6; 6:15; cf. Eph. 2:11-22). The lesson Peter learned when he was sent to Cornelius surely sums up the New Testament position: 'I now realise . . . that God does not show favouritism but accepts men from every nation . . .' (Acts 10:34f.).

On a wider canvas we have Paul's assertion at Athens that God made every nation of men from one man so that, as a Greek poet had said, 'We are his offspring' (Acts 17:26-28). Wherever there is a 'man', that man is God's offspring and, therefore, a being of equal worth with all other men. And, since God shows no partiality as between Jew and non-Jew and requires his servants not to show favouritism (Jas. 2:1-9), we can conclude that he requires us, his servants today, to let no barrier of culture or race hinder the proclamation of the gospel.

Differences there are, and differences between people there will always be—differences in language, in the colour of skin, in culture, social status and values. Faith in Christ does not change a Greek into a Hebrew any more than it changes a slave into a freeman or a woman into a man! But it ought to enable us to accept one another with our differences and to recognise the worth of one another as persons.

Those called to serve the Lord in mission should see a potential harvest wherever and among whatever people they happen to be at any particular time. They must divest themselves of every vestige of racial and cultural prejudice. They must never regard themselves or the cultural mores of their own people as superior to those of the people they seek to win. Like the gospel itself, they must be able to transcend every difference and minister without favouritism to whomever the Lord is pleased to bring into their sphere of service.

Appendix B
Women and mission

It is often said that women are the backbone of modern missionary work. Male Christians are even castigated for being less willing to serve as missionaries than are their sisters in Christ. It is apparently true that there are about twice as many women as men in mission! A cynic might say that the male response is, 'Lord, here am I . . . send my sister!'

Whatever the facts about our day and age, our concern here is to examine the picture as it is found in Scripture.

The Old Testament background

It is important to notice that women had a prophetic ministry in ancient Israel. A prophet, it will be remembered, was primarily a 'caller' or an 'announcer', a messenger who spoke to men on behalf of God the Lord. Moses' sister Miriam was a prophetess (Exod. 15:20), and so was Deborah, who in addition even served as a national leader or judge (Judg. 4:4). Isaiah's wife was also called a prophetess and was almost certainly a prophet in her own right (Isa. 8:3).

Even more interesting is the case of Huldah, to whom Hilkiah and other officials were sent by King Josiah 'to enquire of the Lord' about the contents and meaning of the Book of the Law which had been found in the temple (2 Kgs. 22:13f.). Huldah did what was asked of her and as a result received God's message and delivered it to the king and those men involved with him in ruling the land. She was a prophet, a spokeswoman for God, and neither the men to whom she spoke nor the divine author of the record that has come down to us indicate any incongruity in the fact that a woman was God's messenger to males. Indeed, the fact that the Holy Spirit has seen fit to record the incident without negative comment is surely tacit approval of what had happened.

In harmony with this is the prophecy of Joel, which finds ful-filment in the new order inaugurated at Pentecost:

> And afterwards, I will pour out my Spirit on all people. Your sons and daughters will prophesy . . . Even on my servants, both men and women, I will pour out my Spirit in those days (Joel 2:28f.; cf. Acts 2:17f.).

While it is clear that prophetic ministry was open to women in the Old Testament era, the number of those actually called to it was comparatively small. The fact that many prophets simply spoke as and when the Lord called them to do so meant that it was reasonably possible for women as well as men to be among those so called.

The parallel ministries of priests and of full-time prophets were different matters because they involved full-time employ-ment of an institutionalised nature and as such were neither suitable for nor open to women. What is not always realised is that in the ancient world life expectation was short—possibly aver-aging about 30 years for females—and that because of the huge loss of life through war and pestilence the replenishment of the human population was always the top priority. This necessari-ly restricted the activities of women to family life and in some mea-sure accounts for their low profile in Israelite religious leadership.

Women witnessing for Jesus

In general Jesus put women on a equal footing with men. He demanded the same standards of spirituality and morality from both. He required faith and accepted devotion and service from both.

It is, of course, true that our Lord chose twelve men to be his disciples and as such to become apostles or missionaries. Clearly, however, in a world in which wisdom was regarded as a male preserve and in which it would have been contrary to decorum to mix males and females in an itinerating team, he appointed or commissioned twelve men. By itself, however, this is not proof that he intended that for ever thereafter men and not women should serve as missionaries.

The Gospels record two significant instances of our Lord using women to communicate the truth about himself. The first is that of the woman he met at Sychar's well in Samaria. She went into the town inviting the people to come and meet the one she had met and who had identified himself to her as the Messiah. Many heeded her and, meeting Jesus, believed on him (John 4:25-30; 39-41). While the record does not say specifically that Jesus 'sent' her back to the town, it does juxtapose the conversion of the Samaritans with his teaching on the immediacy of missionary opportunity and on the way in which one missionary reaps where another has sown (vv. 35-38). The faith of the Samaritans clearly resulted from the missionary work of the woman as well as from that of the disciples and of the Lord himself.

The second incident occurred on the day of our Lord's resurrection. He 'sent' Mary Magdalene to his disciples—'Go . . . to my brothers and tell them, I am returning to my Father and your Father, to my God and your God.' And Mary did exactly what he commissioned her to do: she 'went to the disciples with the news: "I have seen the Lord!" And she told them that he had said these things to her' (John 20:17-18).

Mary was a bearer of news—the good news—that the Lord had risen. She was a servant sent by the Lord, in effect a missionary, the very first person to proclaim the triumphant message of the resurrection.

Women missionaries in the early Church

The outpouring of the Holy Spirit at Pentecost fulfilled our Lord's promise that the disciples would receive power that would make them effective witnesses for him (Acts 1:8). Those who waited and prayed for the fulfilment were both male and female (Acts 1:14), and there is absolutely nothing in the record of Pentecost to suggest that power for witness (i.e. mission) was given to men and not to women, or that it was given in greater measure to men than to women. Indeed, if that had been the case, Peter could not have quoted verbatim the words of Joel that daughters as well as sons would prophesy, and that God would pour his Spirit on his servants, both men and women.

At the inauguration of church life, then, women were given a role in mission—they were to be spokespersons for God. In keeping with this is the fact that in Paul's discussion of the place of spiritual gifts or charismata there is no hint that the Holy Spirit bestowed those gifts on men alone. Indeed, he asserts that the manifestations of the Spirit are given 'to each one, just as he determines' (1 Cor. 12:7-11). He says that the gifts are given for the benefit of the body to which, he asserts, all believers, all who have been baptised by the Spirit into Christ belong (1 Cor. 12:12f.).

Now if the gifts are bestowed on each member of the body of Christ, and if women are members of that body, then the gifts must be bestowed on them as well as on men. If this were not the case women would not be in the body, would not be Christians and would have no hope of salvation—a totally preposterous - proposition!

Several of the gifts Paul lists involve what we would call 'communication skills'. The 'message of wisdom' and 'the message of knowledge' are certainly such, as is the gift of prophecy, the significance of which is hotly disputed in some circles today.

That prophecy is among the gifts bestowed by the Lord on his church can hardly be questioned (cf. 1 Cor. 11:4-5; 12:28; 13:2;14:1-39; Eph. 4:11). However, prophecy in the New Testament, as indeed in the Old, is not, and must not be construed as, basically or essentially predictive: it is the delivery of God's word, whether that word relates to the present, to the past or to the future. That it entails positive teaching and pastoral ministry and, indeed, that it has an evangelistic impact is absolutely clear from Paul's descriptions of it:

everyone who prophesies speaks to men for their strengthening, encouragement and comfort (1 Cor. 14:3).

if an unbeliever or someone who does not understand comes in [i.e. to a meeting of Christians] while everybody is prophesying, he will be convinced by all that he is a sinner . . . So he will fall down and worship God, exclaiming, 'God is really among you!' (1 Cor. 14:24f.).

We also know that the four daughters of Philip were prophets, butwe have no information about how or to whom they ministered (Acts 21:8f.). As prophets they must have spoken and taught God's word in and around Caesarea where they lived.

In the Acts of the Apostles we meet Priscilla, the wife of Aquila, who with her husband made a marvellous contribution to the apostolic mission. On half of the occasions on which this couple is mentioned Priscilla's name occurs first, suggesting that, if she was not the dominant partner in the work of mission, she was certainly not in a subordinate role. In fact she shared with Aquila in teaching the things of God to Apollos—a man! (Acts 18:26). Paul thought of her as his fellow worker just as much as was her husband (Rom. 16:3). He had a similar view of Euodia and Syntyche who, despite the disagreement then affecting them, had been at Paul's side contending for the gospel (Phil. 4:2f.).

An interesting remark among Paul's greetings at the end of his letter to the Romans demands particular consideration: 'Greet Andronicus and Junias, my relatives who have been in prison with me. They are outstanding among the apostles, and they were in Christ before I was' (Rom. 16:7).

The 1611 Authorised Version reads, 'Salute Andronicus and Junia, my kinsmen, and my fellowprisoners, who are of note among the apostles . . .' Junias (NIV) is a masculine name, while Junia (AV) is a feminine one referring to a woman. The original Greek is not definite either way because, as the object of the verb 'greet', both the masculine and the feminine names take the same form. If the AV is correct in translating the name as Junia, we have a reference to a couple, presumably man and wife, who worked with Paul in his apostolic/missionary team and who had actually been imprisoned with him.

In earlier times some exegetes understood Paul to be referring to a woman who worked with him and his colleagues as an apostle or missionary. Thus John Chrysostom (c.347-407 AD) said, 'Oh! How great is this woman that she should be even counted worthy of the appellation of an apostle.' Calvin, who also thought the reference was to a woman, got round what for him must have been a difficult idea (a female apostle) by arguing that here Paul was using the word apostle in an unusual way. Nonetheless he maintained that Paul was extending the meaning of the word to include all (i.e. men and women) 'who do not only instruct one church, but for the publishing of the gospel every where do bestow their labour. They, therefore, who, by carrying the doctrine of salvation hither and thither did plant churches are generally in this place called apostles' (*Commentary on Romans*, Beveridge Edition, Edinburgh, 1844, p.421). For Calvin, Junia, a woman, was a gospel-proclaiming and a church-planting missionary.

While the sex of Junia or Junias is and must remain somewhat uncertain, it is hard to avoid the feeling that the translators of our more modern versions have come to their tasks with the presupposition that the apostles were all male and that any reference to a woman as being notable among the apostles had to be avoided—the masculine form of the name Junias had, therefore, to be used. Ancient records suggest, however, that the masculine form was rather rare at the time, while the feminine form, Junia, was common, a fact which rather tilts the balance of probability in favour of the companion of Andronicus being a woman and, if so, quite probably his wife.

The priesthood of all believers

In the Old Testament era Israel was served by a corps of priests, one of whose duties related to the presentation of the offerings and sacrifices of the people before the Lord. As the writer to the Hebrews says, the high priest 'is appointed to represent them [i.e. human beings] in matters related to God, to offer gifts and sacrifices for sins' (5:1). This role, as the same writer so carefully explains, has been fulfilled by Christ, the ultimate high priest, whose offering of himself was a 'once for all' affair that needs no repetition (9:24-28; 10:26). There is therefore no need now for priests to mediate between men and God. He, the Lord Jesus, is our high priest and is the one and only mediator between God and men (1 Tim. 2:5).

That said, it has to be noted that the New Testament speaks of the community of believers as a 'priesthood'—'a holy priesthood' and 'a royal priesthood' (1 Pet. 2:5,9) and as 'a kingdom and priests' (Rev. 1:6; 5:10). During the Reformation these passages were used by Luther and others to counter the priestcraft and the priestly control of the medieval church which they wanted to reform. They stressed that, in the new order in Christ, all believers are priests and individually each has direct access to God through the one mediator, the risen Lord himself. Each is to offer himself or herself to God as a living sacrifice (Rom. 12:1f.) and each is to offer to God a sacrifice of praise (Heb. 13:15).

What is not often realised is that the role of the Levitical priesthood in ancient Israel had another dimension which was made clear when Moses blessed the various tribes just before his death. The tribe of Levi, which had been set apart from the others to perform religious functions and from which the priests were drawn, had as its primary function not the offering of sacrifice but the guarding of God's word and covenant and the teaching of his law to Israel:

> . . . he watched over your word and guarded your covenant. He teaches your precepts to Jacob and your law to Israel. He offers incense before you and whole burnt offerings on your altar (Deut. 33:9b,10a, but note all of vv. 8-11).

The primary priestly functions of guarding the word or truth of God and of teaching it to the rising generations does not seem to be abrogated in the same way as is that of offering sacrifices. Indeed it is actually endorsed and passed on to the church and especially to missionaries in our Lord's great commission:

... go and make disciples of all nations, baptising them in the name of the Father and of the Son and of the Holy Spirit and teaching them to obey everything I have commanded you (Matt. 28:19).

Since all believers are priests, then, surely, all believers share the responsibility to make disciples, to bring converts into church life through baptism, and to teach those converts the full gamut of what our Lord himself taught. We, all believers together, constitute 'a holy priesthood' or 'a royal priesthood' (1 Pet. 2:5,9). And 'all believers' includes those who are female, for all without distinction, male and female, have been baptised into the one body and are one in Christ Jesus (1 Cor. 12:12f.; Gal. 3:26-29). We are one in our privileges and we are one in missionary responsibility.

Conclusion

Christian women cannot opt out of mission or say that it is a work meant for men. They, with their male fellow believers, must face up to and respond to the obligation resting on all.

Christians are to be witnesses for the Lord and must be willing to go into missionary work when he calls them to do so. As Calvin, believing the name Junia in Romans 16:7 to refer to a woman, asserted, the word apostle (i.e. sent-out one or missionary) is extended to include all (i.e. male and female) who, labouring for the publishing of the gospel, carry the doctrine of salvation hither and thither and plant churches.

There are—there must be—women apostles in the sense of sent-out persons, women who serve as missionaries, who proclaim salvation, who teach those who have come to faith in Christ and who may, as Calvin's words suggest, be agents for the planting of churches.

It is the Lord's prerogative to bestow the gifts necessary for mission and to call those he so gifts to serve him in mission. It is our responsibility, whether we are women or men, to obey that call when it comes to us.